Decorative Plates

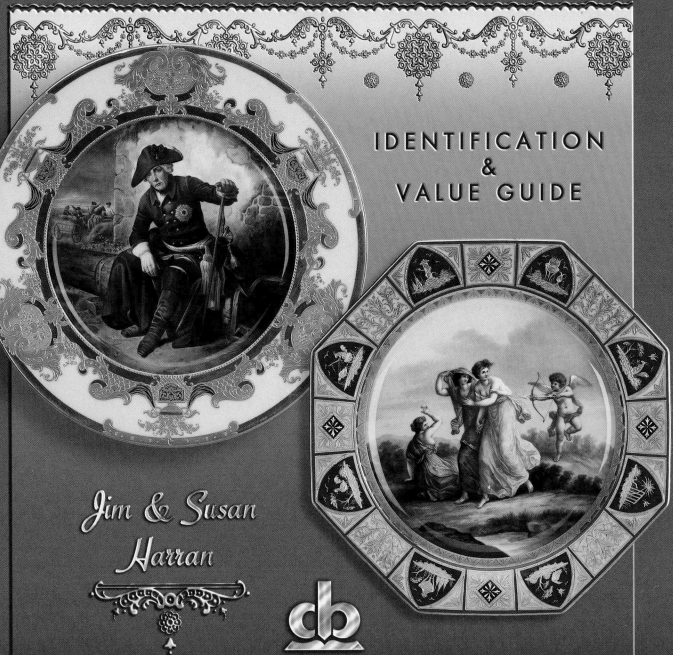

IDENTIFICATION & VALUE GUIDE

Jim & Susan Harran

COLLECTOR BOOKS
A Division of Schroeder Publishing Co., Inc.

On the front cover:
Top right: Limoges, Comte D'Artoise, c. 1930s, artist signed "Leon." 9"; hand-painted purple and white flowers with heavy gold border. $200.00 – 250.00.
Top left: Unmarked, French, c. 1900 – 1920, artist signed "Amelie." Square, 8½"; hand-painted birds painted on a diagonal. $75.00 – 100.00.
Middle: Royal Vienna style, underglaze shield mark, c. 1870s. Octagonal, 9¾"; "Amor's Revanche" in script, Cupid trying to shoot his arrow at a young lady while her friends attempt to protect her form his advances, wonderful border with 16 differents painting in heavy gold and enameling. $1,000.00 – 1,200.00.
Bottom right: Portrait. KPM, painted outside factory by Dresden decorator Grace H. Bishop, c. 1890s. 8"; adorable portrait of Zuleika, cobalt border with pearl jeweling, gold beads, and gilt flowers and leaves. $800.00 – 1,000.00. (See mark #57).
Bottom left: Royal Vienna style, underglaze shield mark, c. 1890s. 9½"; Art Nouveau, gold ground with raised gold leaves framed by an array of hand-painted green grape leaves; portrait of lovely lady named Epheu, who has long black hair in which there is garland of grape leaves. $1,400.00 – 1,500.00.

On the back cover:
KPM, painted outside factory, c. 1870. 10⅓"; entitled "Friedrich der Grosse nach Hallin," hand-painted portrait of King Frederick in his military uniform, lavish gilt border. $1,200.00 – 1,300.00.

Cover design by Beth Summers
Book design by Barry Buchanan

COLLECTOR BOOKS
P.O. Box 3009
Paducah, Kentucky 42002-3009

www.collectorbooks.com

Copyright © 2008 Jim and Susan Harran

The current values in this book should be used only as a guide. They are not intended to set prices, which vary from one section of the country to another. Auction prices as well as dealer prices vary greatly and are affected by condition as well as demand. Neither the authors nor the publisher assumes responsibility for any losses that might be incurred as a result of consulting this guide.

738.2

Searching for a Publisher?

We are always looking for people knowledgeable within their fields. If you feel that there is a real need for a book on your collectible subject and have a large comprehensive collection, contact Collector Books.

Proudly printed and bound in the United States of America

CONTENTS

DEDICATION

To Andrea and Joey Sabato and Gracie, the newest member of our family.

ACKNOWLEDGMENTS

First and foremost, we'd like to thank the members of the staff at Collector Books. If it had not been for our publisher, Bill Schroeder; our editor, Gail Ashburn; and her assistant, Amy Sullivan, this book would not have been possible. We appreciate the beautiful cover design by Beth Summers and the book design by Barry Buchanan. The staff at Collector Books is professional, talented, and always helpful.

We would like to express our appreciation to those collectors and dealers who so generously gave of their time and knowledge to make this book a reality. We are indebted to Brenda Pardee of Bloomfield, New York. This is the third book that Brenda has helped us with, and we greatly appreciate her generosity. Brenda supplied us with many photographs from her plate collection, including some wonderful examples of historical and romantic Staffordshire.

Once again, we would like to thank Mary Davis of Rock Hill, South Carolina, who also sent us photographs for our book on cups and saucers. Mary has a lovely collection of cobalt blue plates. We appreciate the professional quality of her photographs.

Many thanks to our good friend Richard Rendall of Cincinnati, Ohio, for sending us some photographs from his fine plate collection. We always enjoy sharing information about hand-painted porcelain with Richard. Richard has written a beautiful book, entitled *Hand Painted Porcelain Plates* and published by Schiffer Books, that has been most helpful to us.

Special thanks to Joan and Ken Oates from Marshall, Michigan, for sending us photographs from their collection. Joan graciously sent us a complimentary copy of her fifth book on Phoenix Bird china, and it was helpful to us.

We would like to thank Marvin and Matt Baer of the Ivory Tower Inc. in Ridgwood, New Jersey, for letting us come into their booth during a show to photograph some of their outstanding Oriental plates. Oriental pieces of this quality and condition are rare, and we thank Marvin and Matt for sharing them with us.

We are grateful to Barbara Jones of Fairfax, Virginia, for sending us photographs of some of her top-quality service plates. We thank Yuji Anzai of Asaka Fine Arts, in San Francisco, California, for sending us photos of interesting Oriental plates. Thanks also to Ivo Ispani and T. J. Van Der Horst of Duomo Antiques, in Carversville, Pennsylvania, for allowing us to photograph some of their Oriental and Italian plates. Our appreciation is extended to Wilbur and Aunalie Robinson of Sunbury, Ohio, for sending us a photo from their collection. Thanks to Patricia Marsico and Jeanette Mostowicz of Marsmost Antiques in Netcong, New Jersey, for allowing us to photograph their Danish Christmas plates.

Lastly, we again thank Todd Robertson, owner of Sure Service Photo in Neptune City, New Jersey, and the members of his staff, Barbara and Marie, for their support. They were never too busy to process our film in a professional manner.

ABOUT THE AUTHORS

Susan and Jim Harran, antiques dealers of A Moment in Time, specialize in English and Continental porcelains and antique cups and saucers. The Harrans have authored five books, entitled *Collectible Cups and Saucers* books I, II, and III, *Dresden Porcelain Studios,* and *Meissen Porcelain*. They write feature articles for various antiques publications and have a monthly column in *AntiqueWeek* entitled "The World of Ceramics." Susan is a member of the Antique Appraisal Association of America Inc., and they are both members of the Antiques & Collectibles Dealer Association. The Harrans display their antiques at some of the top antiques shows in the country. They also do business on the Internet. Their website is www.tias.com/stores/amit. The Harrans enjoy traveling around the country to keep abreast of trends in the antiques marketplace. They reside in Neptune, New Jersey.

Almost every antiques lover has a few decorative plates in his or her collection. We have been buying and selling plates for the 25 years we've been in the antiques business. We find them fascinating and have kept a few special plates for our own personal collection.

Some of the finest-quality artwork appears on plates. The surface of a plate is so flat and smooth that wonderfully detailed painting can be achieved. Once fired, the colors are permanent. A porcelain plate painted in 1800 will look exactly the same 200 years later. Oil painting tends to darken with age, and watercolors fade.

Beautiful examples of decorative plates have been made by almost every porcelain company in the world in a variety of subjects and in all price ranges. Collectors of a certain manufacturer, such as Royal Worcester, consider plates to be examples of the company's finest work and eagerly hunt for them.

There are a variety of subjects found on decorative plates. Top of the line are portrait plates which can show off the painter's artistic skill. Landscapes, animals, birds, flowers, and fruit are the most common subjects found on plates, and some are extremely lifelike and beautifully painted. Collectors interested in a special subject are sure to find a number of plates to enjoy.

Plates have been used to decorate and beautify homes since early times. They are easy to display, as they are much smaller than canvas paintings. Plates can be displayed in cabinets, on shelves, or hung on walls.

Plates can be found in all price ranges. The best examples made by Meissen, Royal Vienna, Sevres, Royal Worcester, and Satsuma are rare and expensive, and many are in museums today. More moderately priced plates painted by one of the factories at Limoges or decorating studios in Paris, Dresden, or Vienna, the popular Staffordshire blue and white transferware, and Nippon are affordable and readily available in the marketplace today. Finally, there are a variety of inexpensive plates, such as the interesting Japanese Phoenix Bird china and American home-decorated dinnerware.

The purpose of this book is to include information and realistic prices for a wide range of plates that are readily found in the marketplace, from good transfer-print decoration to fine-quality hand-painted decoration. We have included over 800 color photographs.

Our first chapter includes historical background on early ceramic art, the development of tableware, and plates for display. We explain the different types of plates, such as chargers, service plates, game and fish sets, oyster plates, and commemorative plates. We discuss the variety of subjects found on plates and include information about influential canvas portrait artists. Finally, we explain how a plate is made.

Our book is then organized by country or geographic area. The first of these chapters includes American plates. We discuss the development of American Belleek in Tren-ton, New Jersey, which was considered one of the highest achievements of the American porcelain industry. We also discuss Deldare art pottery, Pickard china, and the popular hobby of American china painting.

Our chapter on English plates includes examples of some of the most eagerly collected plates, Staffordshire blue and white transferware. We discuss some of the top English makers of plates and provide photographs and prices of representative examples.

In our chapter on French plates, we discuss the importance and popularity of Limoges porcelain. Limoges was the center of hard-paste porcelain production in France, and at one time there were as many as 48 companies in Limoges. We include information on the most well known of these companies. We discuss Paris porcelains and include popular studios. We also try to clarify misconceptions about Paris porcelains. We include other French makers, including Sevres, the luxury name in French porcelain.

In our chapter on German plates, we discuss Dresden, the center of the Romantic movement in Germany. There were more than 200 painting shops in Dresden, and many produced beautiful hand-painted plates. We discuss the work of several of the most prolific studios. We discuss the top German porcelain companies, including Meissen and KPM.

In our chapter on other European plates, we attempt to clarify the confusion over Royal Vienna plates. We discuss the actual company, its closure in 1864, and the Royal Vienna style that developed in the late nineteenth century. We discuss the best and the worst examples of Royal Vienna style and the confusion over the shield mark. Companies in Czechoslovakia, Denmark, Hungary, Italy, and Russia are also included.

Our chapter on Oriental plates includes information on Chinese Export porcelain. We briefly discuss the development of Japanese ceramics and include examples of Imari, Kutani, Nippon, and Satsuma, which is one of the most treasured and sought-after porcelains. We discuss the affordable blue and white Phoenix Bird china.

Our last chapter provides useful information for the collector, and we also include a helpful marks section and an index.

Many print publications and many Internet sources supplied helpful information, and these sources are acknowledged in the bibliography. We hope this book will make it easier for the beginning as well as the advanced collector, dealer, and appraiser identify and price decorative plates. We realize that in a book of this nature and scope, some degree of error is unavoidable, and we apologize in advance.

We would appreciate hearing your comments, and our address is below. If you would like a reply, please include a self-addressed stamped envelope.

Jim and Susan Harran
208 Hemlock Drive
Neptune, NJ 07753

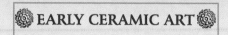

EARLY CERAMIC ART

Man developed a form of clay as early as 26,000 BC. It consisted of mammoth fat and bone mixed with bone ash and local mud. It was discovered that if the substance was molded and dried in the sun, it would form a brittle, heat-resistant material. This began ceramic art. By 13,000 BC, ceramic vessels were used to hold everyday foods and beverages. In 6,000 BC, ceramic firing was discovered in Ancient Greece. The Greek pottery Pithoi was developed and used for storage, burial, and art. During the same period, the Turks established a pottery-making center in the village of Hacilar. Popular motifs were flowers shaped like Maltese crosses, and human and animal figures.

The Chinese discovered how to make porcelain around 600 A.D. They had a large supply of kaolin clay, which was the major ingredient. They developed kiln techniques and glazing processes and created hard-paste porcelain. When trade routes opened from Europe to China in the 1300s, porcelain objects, including dinner plates, became a great passion for European nobility.

It was not until the early eighteenth century that porcelain was finally discovered in Europe. In 1701 the Saxon king, Augustus II, heard of a young alchemist, Johann Friedrich Böttger (1682 – 1719), who boasted that he could produce gold from base metals. Augustus II took him into custody and ordered him to produce gold. After Böttger's experiments failed at the Saxon court, Augustus II placed him under the supervision of Ehrenfried Walther von Tschirnhaus (1651 – 1708), who was a Saxon mathematician and physicist of international renown. Their task was to invent "white gold" similar to that made by the Chinese. Augustus II ordered Böttger and his team to work in isolation in the medieval fortress, Albrechtsberg, the castle in Meissen.

In 1707 Böttger was brought back to the castle in Dresden to live in a closely guarded laboratory in the Venus Tower. It was in this fume laden, unhealthy lab that Böttger, assisted by his fellow workers, finally developed the first European hard-paste porcelain.

On March 28, 1709, Böttger sent a message to Augustus II. It informed the king that he had invented a white porcelain as good as the Chinese one if not superior. On January 23, 1710, it was proudly announced in four languages that the elector of Saxony and King of Poland planned to establish a porcelain manufactory that would make porcelain equaling that made in Eastern Asia. The manufactory began operation on June 6, 1710, in Meissen, in the Gothic fortress of Albrechtsberg.

DEVELOPMENT OF TABLEWARE

Around 2,000 BC, in ancient Crete, meals were served on pottery plates which were usually brightly decorated with abstract designs. Wealthy families in Egypt had a variety of tableware made from gold, silver, bronze, and pottery. In ancient Rome food was served for the royalty on a discus, which is a large circular plate. It was made from silver, bronze, or pewter and was elaborately carved. Individual plates were made from bronze, pewter, or red earthenware called Samian ware.

SAMIAN WARE

Samian ware was the fine tableware of the early Roman Empire made from the first century to the third century AD. The word *Samian* comes from the Greek island of Samos, where the ware originated. Wherever the Romans settled, they took Samian ware with them.

The red earthenware was used for all kinds of domestic crockery from cups, plates, bowls to vases and cooking pots. The red clay was covered with a fine transparent glaze. Some pieces were plain with highly polished surfaces. Others were finely decorated, either with patterns made by pressing molded stamps into the soft clay before firing or slip decorated with raised dots and lines. Samian ware was mass-produced, and the finished pieces often had a manufacturer's stamp. There are many examples of this early tableware in museums today.

TRENCHERS

After the Norman Conquest in 1066, the trencher came into being. It was a small rectangular or square flat object that was given to each person at the table. Some trenchers were made of wood. Many of the first trenchers were made from a specially baked whole meal bread, which was kept for four days and then trimmed to shape with a special trencher knife. It was about six inches across and hard enough to hold hot food. The word trencher is derived from the French verb *trenchier*, or "to cut." After the trencher was used, it would be covered with bits of food and given to the dogs or to the poor.

In the United States, handmade square or oblong wooden trenchers were used by the colonists for more than a century. From an oblong trencher, two persons sometimes ate in common. Two children frequently ate from the same trencher. These wooden trenchers gradu-

ally evolved into plates by first having a hollow turned on them and then having the square profile removed to leave the plate round as we know it today.

Soon after the plate had reached its present form, wood began to be used less. Rising living standards in the sixteenth and seventeenth centuries meant more people could afford metals. Since solid silver was extremely expensive, many households used pewter as a substitute. It was much softer than silver. Even a moderately hard cut with a knife would scratch its surface, so it was in need of constant maintenance.

Ceramic plates gradually displaced wood and pewter

plates in the seventeenth century, although those types were still used at different levels of society until the early nineteenth century. Since then, pottery and porcelain plates have been universal.

A major English contribution to the eighteenth century dining table was cream-colored earthenware developed by Josiah Wedgwood in the 1760s. It was pale enough to resemble porcelain and was called creamware. It instantly became popular worldwide.

After the development of porcelain in Europe by Meissen, porcelain became the first choice of tableware. It was the perfect material, because once it was fired it was much harder and durable than earthenware or stoneware. It held its shape better in firing. Unlike metal and wood, porcelain did not impart a flavor to foods served in it. In the nineteenth century, improved production and transfer-printing techniques made porcelain more affordable for everyone.

Still life showing pewter plate, postcard.

PLATES FOR DISPLAY

"There's hardly a plate that I can walk by without picking it up, bringing it over, and examining every detail…And I don't just use plates to serve meals. I hang them on my walls, stack them on a side table, display them in a hutch, use them to brighten up a dark corner. They are just as versatile as artwork — perhaps even more so, since you don't have to worry about frames." (Mary Engelbreit, Plates)

Plate display, Marken, Series 178 #3061.

ANCIENT TIMES

When man required containers for everyday use and storage, he fashioned them out of clay. In his need to make the plates and bowls waterproof, he developed various nonporous glazes to cover them. He observed that colored glazes beautified the objects. Pleased with the attractive results, he decided to model purely decorative pieces.

The decorative possibilities of the plate were recognized by the Chinese over a thousand years ago. They produced pottery plates with colorful figures of dragons, birds and flowers in relief.

In the third through sixth centuries AD, decorative plates were made from red slipware in provinces located in what is now modern Tunisia in North Africa. Scenes from the Bible, sporting events, nature, and daily life were decorated on plates, which were exported throughout the Roman Empire.

LUSTER WARE

In the early ninth century, potters in Mesopotamia, a region that includes modern-day Iraq, were inspired by Chinese wares, and they tried to imitate them. The first types of wares were tan or red earthenwares covered with a tin glaze. In an effort to simulate metals, potters developed the luster technique, and during the next 300 years, this method of decoration spread through Islamic countries, reaching Spain in the thirteenth or fourteenth centuries.

Arab plate sellers, postcard, Collection Ideale P. S.

BLUE AND WHITE

The Mongols ruled China in the early fourteenth century. They had ties with the Islamic leaders of the Middle East. This relationship produced the first market for blue and white wares. The vivid cobalt pigment mined in Persia was favored in that region. Cobalt was exported to China and used to decorate porcelain goods sold to the Islamic traders. This new blue and white decoration caught on in the Chinese domestic market as well, replacing the traditional monochrome, or one-color, wares. Blue and white decoration had such tremendous impact on the porcelain trade that it dominated the international market for 300 years.

MAJOLICA

A majolica-style pottery originated over 20,000 years ago in North Africa, where the technique of adding an opaque tin glaze to baked clay was introduced. In the eighth century when the Moors joined together to conquer Spain, they brought the secrets of majolica with them, and it began to influence Spanish art.

During the Renaissance, Spaniards exported their version of tin-glazed pottery to Italy from Majorca, an island shipping port in the Mediterranean Sea. The Italians called the colorful pottery *maiolica*, as this was their spelling of the Spanish island's name.

It was in Florence that the full artistic potential of majolica was first appreciated. Famous fifteenth-century sculptor Luca della Robbia wanted to add color to his creations, and the new material was perfect. By the end of the sixteenth century, every region in Italy was making tin-glazed earthenware.

Many large decorative majolica plates were made for display on the walls of Italian homes. Potters produced plates, decorated with family crests, that had Biblical scenes, portraits of kings, and events in history. Some majolica plates were covered completely with a single scene. This type of decoration was known as *istoriato* ("history painting") and was made at Urbino, Italy.

Sacred plates for weddings were painted by Italian artists. These were called marriage plates and were hung upon the walls and looked upon with superstitious awe. They were painted in polychrome, and their chief designs were biblical subjects.

In seventeenth century Italy, large plates were often made and decorated by priests. Priest Antonio Maria Cuzio, like other dignitaries of the church, amused himself by making ceramics. He made a number of large plates in Pavia, Italy, decorating them with biblical or classical themes.

DELFT

Delft became an important pottery center in Holland in 1605. Delftware was exported all over the world. Many chargers and plates were made to hang as pictures. For special commissions, outside artists were called in to do the decorating. Subjects were landscapes, portraits, and historical events.

Portrait of little Dutch girl on Delft plate, postcard, PBF 6998.

A display of plates on a shelf in a primitive farmhouse, postcard Druck von E. Nister, Nurnburg.

VICTORIAN RACK PLATES

For centuries, plates have been hung on walls and placed on tops of mantels, cupboards, and dressers in farm and country homes. In Victorian times clutter was the rage, and every spot had to have something on it. Plates were not only hung on a wall but often a narrow shelf was built around the room a few inches below the molding as a rack for plates. These plates were called rack plates in England and Canada.

MODERN TIMES

Today, plate collecting is more popular than ever. Plates are hung on walls, displayed in cabinets, and arranged on shelves. There are a variety of different stands that can be purchased to display them.

"I enjoy hanging pretty plates in a grouping on a wall and have noticed that many of the decorating publications show them even in bedrooms or bathrooms. This Fall, we grouped the dishes with nut themes in a large wicker tray…for the center of the coffee table. We put a few on plate stands… Of course, the poinsettia plates reigned for the holidays." (Sandra Hawke, "Collectors Favor Hand-Painted China Pieces," Spring 2002 Home Improvement Show)

Thanksgiving plate, postcard, printed in Germany, No. 51670.

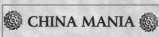

CHINA MANIA

Porcelain collecting dates back to the Turkish sultans, who had famous acquisitions of Chinese porcelain as early as the fifteenth century. Their great passion is shown by large collections in the Museum of Constantinople, which contains about 10,000 pieces of porcelain, some pieces dating from the Sung Dynasty (960 – 1279).

Louis XIV, the Sun King, built the Trianon of Porcelain in the park of Versailles in the seventeenth century. He dedicated it to his mistress, the Marquise de Monteopan, as a teahouse. This teahouse introduced porcelain cabinets, or galleries, to the European courts.

The success of the Meissen manufactory after 1720 inflamed Augustus II's passion for collecting porcelain. He bought a small palace in 1717 across the Elbe River from his Dresden residence, which he called the Japanese Palace. He gave orders to Meissen for many pieces of porcelain to be displayed in his palace.

Monarchs and royalty continued their traditional practice of collecting and displaying porcelain throughout the eighteenth century, but porcelain was still beyond the means of the average citizen. In the nineteenth century, improved production and decorating techniques made porcelain more affordable.

Queen Mary of Teck (1867 – 1953) was an ardent collector of china. Her love for china was partly responsible for the evolution of a new article of furniture—the china cabinet with glass doors. Choice pieces of porcelain could now be displayed in a safe and protected environment.

The American colonists also appreciated good china and were eager to possess the best. It was not uncommon to send special orders for complete dinner services to the Orient. When a ship laden with china was lured by wreckers to destruction on the Barnegat shores of New Jersey, the "beach china," as it was called, found a ready and profitable market.

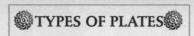

TYPES OF PLATES

DESSERT PLATES

The main standby of eighteenth century English porcelain factories was not dinner services but dessert services. This was a class of porcelain neglected by the Chinese potters. Dessert, which in the eighteenth and nineteenth centuries usually meant fruit, was eaten from richly decorated plates. They rarely matched the dinner service. The dessert service market was a very important one in England, and many of the single plates found in collections today were originally part of such services.

CAKE PLATES

Cake plates are usually about 11" wide and often have two handles to ease in serving. They are almost always round in shape, because cakes are usually round. The round cakes we know today were descended from ancient bread. They were made by hand and shaped into round balls and baked on hearthstones or in low shallow pans. The finished product normally relaxed into rounded shapes. Ancient breads and cakes were sometimes used in religious ceremonies. They were made into round shapes to symbolize the cyclical nature of life, specifically the sun and moon.

Cake plates are eagerly collected today and make attractive wall decorations. Collectors look for hand-painted Limoges, Nippon, and Pickard plates, as well as the less-expensive transfer-decorated plates made in Germany and England.

CHARGERS

Chargers are large round flat plates ranging in size from 11" to 20½" in diameter. They have always been used for display. In Italy in the seventeenth century, the early majolica charger or show dish was about 17½" wide and very popular. The shape of the molded charger was inspired by baroque models in silver.

In seventeenth century England, blue-dash chargers were produced. These have borders of hand-painted blue dashes. The earliest were painted with fruit and floral designs. Around 1650, a series of chargers with paintings of kings or national heroes was begun with a portrait of Charles I.

Blue-dash chargers were used to decorate the home and were hung on walls or placed on court cupboards. A court cupboard is a moveable sideboard or buffet, on which chargers and other articles of luxury were displayed on special occasions. They were owned by wealthy families and used for the display of silver, Delftware, and other treasured items.

SERVICE PLATES

A 1940 Spode dinnerware catalog produced by Copeland & Thompson, Inc., NY, defines a service plate as a "10 – 10¾" plate, usually with elaborate decoration. It is also called a 'cover plate' or 'place plate.' It is purely decorative and never used for serving food.

"...No food is served directly on the service plate. If a fruit cup is served, it is brought in on a 7" plate and placed on the service plate. If oysters are used, they are served in an oyster plate which is placed on the service plate. When this course is finished, the plate is removed and replaced with a soup plate. And so with the fish plate and entree plate. At the completion of the entree course, the service plate with the entree plate is removed. The roast plate is then placed before the guest."

Service plates are popular with collectors today because they are so decorative and are often embellished with heavy gold. Sets range from 6 to 12 plates.

In an article in the October 10, 2004, *The Daily Item*, of Sunbury, Pennsylvania, Scott Joseph writes that charger plates (service plates) are making a comeback in restaurants. He says that restaurants handle them in several different ways. Some waiters whisk them away as soon as guests are seated. Others let them serve as a large coaster for their cocktail or beverage. Sometimes the appetizer or soup is served on top of the plate and then it is removed for the entrée.

At the fancy Victoria and Albert restaurant in Disney's Grand Floridian hotel, the service plates are removed before any food is served. Wedgwood service plates are used and are decorated with a 24k gold version of the restaurant's logo. If something is put on the plate, the logo gets scratched. If this should happen, it is immediately polished by hand.

GAME AND FISH SETS

Elaborate meals were fashionable among the wealthy during the nineteenth and early twentieth centuries in Europe and America. Four or five separate courses were normally served, and special functions could easily warrant ten or more courses.

Elegant services were especially prized and were used to serve game and fish courses. These sets are very collectible today and include a large platter, 8 to 12 matching plates, and a gravy or sauce boat. Occasionally, ramekins and bone dishes can be found.

The game sets portray animals, and all types of game birds, such as ducks, quail, pheasant, and turkeys, and are often hand painted. The birds are often painted in woodland settings, and some are portrayed dead, hanging from branches. Others are shown flying through the air or swimming in ponds.

The popular fish sets include fresh and saltwater fish

and sometimes depict a different species of fish on each plate. The plates are often decorated with underwater foliage and flowers and are lavishly decorated with gold.

A variety of companies manufactured game and fish sets in England, France, Germany, and in the United States. The greatest number was produced in Limoges, France, especially by Haviland & Company. In America and Canada, Limoges china was considered a status symbol. Professionally decorated Limoges sets range in price from $1,000.00 to $3,500.00, depending on the quality of the porcelain and artwork.

Although table china, the elegant Victorian game services are considered works of art, and many are displayed proudly on the dining room walls of collectors throughout the country. These sets occasionally get broken up, and single plates are collectible as well.

Limoges game set, platter and eight plates, hand-painted game birds.

OYSTER PLATES

The hearty consumption of oysters by Americans during the nineteenth century led to the production of one of the most beautiful Victorian dinnerware items — the oyster plate. Created with great imagination in many fanciful forms by the leading ceramics companies, oyster plates are delightful and eagerly collected today.

Oyster plates were made in a variety of interesting shapes. They can be found round, square, triangular, fan, and crescent shaped, and in animal forms, such as scallops, oysters, and fish. Oyster plates vary in shape, in color, and in number of receptacles, or wells. Many have a deep center well which was used for a lemon wedge,

sauce, other condiment, or if large enough, crackers. The wells range from one to six, two wells being very rare. Larger plates or serving platters were made as well, holding from one to three dozen oysters.

Haviland & Company, organized in 1840, made as many as 60,000 chinaware patterns. Many oyster plates were made by Haviland to complement the dinnerware services. Haviland made oyster plates for certain special people specifically. One of these special people was President Rutherford B. Hayes, who was the nineteenth president of the United States. His term of office was from 1877 to 1881. While in office, he commissioned Haviland to produce a state dinner service for the White House. Part of this set included oyster plates designed by Theodore R. Davis. Each plate contained five oyster wells. The reverse sides of the shells were shown and resembled an outline of a turkey, hence the name "turkey oyster plate."

As the nation's oyster beds were rapidly depleted by the end of the nineteenth century, the oyster reached its pinnacle of popularity. The oyster plate also seemed to reach its peak of fashion between 1880 and 1900. Although once an important part of dinnerware services, the elegant Victorian plates are now displayed proudly on the dining room walls of collectors throughout the world.

Limoges oyster plate, hand-painted purple flowers.

SOUVENIR PLATES

The custom of collecting souvenir plates became popular in the late 1800s. With the introduction of bank holidays in England, it became popular to bring home a pictorial souvenir from any seaside resort, spa town, or place of special interest. These souvenir items were often given to friends as holiday presents.

Pictures were transferred onto items such as mugs, teacups, jugs, and most especially, pierced porcelain plates. Early souvenir plates were either ribbon plates, which had

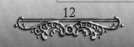

pierced edges through which ribbons could be threaded and tied in bows, or lace plates, which resembled paper doilies. The most popular colors were blue and white. The plates were reasonably priced, and the variety of designs catered to a wide group of collectors.

In the late nineteenth century, a combination of cheap labor, the right kind of clay, and an abundant amount of timber to fuel the kilns led to the porcelain industry springing up in Germany, Austria, and central Europe. These countries produced souvenir plates by the thousands. Pictures of the resorts were sent to plate manufacturers, and orders were placed for the required quantity. Often "A Present From" or "For a Friend" were written on the plate. The practice of buying souvenir plates continues today, but it was at its height between 1880 and 1930.

ALPHABET PLATES

Alphabet plates for teaching young children their letters have been made since the seventeenth century. They were in great demand in England from 1820 to the 1860s, though they were still being made well into the nineteenth century. The earliest plates were creamware with the alphabet embossed around the rim, and a picture with a religious or moral verse or motto. Davenport and Adams made many of these alphabet plates. During Victorian times there were less serious subjects on ABC plates, such as Mother Goose themes and an Every Day Life Series in which Victorian children were pictured doing normal activities.

CHRISTMAS PLATES

Many years ago, the wealthy people of Europe started the custom of giving their servants a Christmas platter heaped with cookies, candy, and fruit. At first the platters were simple scooped-out wooden trenchers. The rich focused their attention on the delicacies on the platter, hoping to bring a little cheer into the lives of the recipients.

The servants looked forward each Christmas to receiving these gifts. Because they couldn't afford many items to decorate their homes, they began hanging their platters on their walls after the food was eaten. They referred to these platters as their Christmas plates.

Soon the servants started showing their plates off to their neighbors, and competition began over who had the most beautiful. When the employers observed this, they began to give more thought to the platter. The rich tried to outdo each other and started to devote more attention to the plate, which was now made of metal and pottery as well as wood.

The best-known Christmas plates are the pure underglaze blue and white editions produced by Bing &

COMMEMORATIVE PLATES

The large flat surface of plates made them a favorite for commemorative ware. Many examples of display plates have been produced since the fifteenth century Italian isoriato ware, where subjects were drawn from historical or biblical events. Election plates to portray candidates were a specialty of Bristol, England in the early eighteenth century.

In England during the early 1900s well known artists were given special commissions to paint commemorative plates and platters. These plates depicted palaces of kings, important national events and special occasions honoring important people. Royal Worcester, Spode, Royal Doulton and Wedgwood quickly realized the popularity of these plates and began to make a variety of them. Wedgwood produced the famous Williamsburg commemorative plates from Queens Ware. The series had twelve plates created by American artist Samuel Chamberlain.

In the United States presidential White House plates are rare and eagerly collected. In an auction by Wiederseim Association in Pennsylvania in March 2006, a set of seven Haviland dessert plates from the dinner service of Ulysses S. Grant sold for $20,182.00. The buyer was the White House Historical Association.

1957 Bing & Grondahl Christmas plate, "Christmas Candles" by Kjeld Bonfils, showing favorite Danish tree ornaments: candles and woven heart baskets filled with treats.

Grondahl and Royal Copenhagen in Denmark. Rosenthal Christmas plates were first issued in 1908. These are of a fine china with Christmas scenes decorated in color on a white ground. These are slightly larger than the Danish plates and are not made in limited editions.

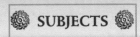 SUBJECTS

There are a variety of subjects found on hand-painted plates. Top of the line are portrait plates, and good examples bring high prices at auctions and shows. The face of a beautiful woman or that of a famous person, such as Napoleon, can show off the painter's artistic skill. Some collectors prefer allegorical or courting scenes. Landscape paintings, animals, and birds can be found. Flowers and fruit are probably the most common subjects found on plates, and some are extremely lifelike and beautifully painted.

> *"Flowers always make people better, happier and more helpful; they are sunshine, food and medicine to the soul."*
> (Luther Burbank, 1849 – 1926)

FLOWERS

Flowers have been among the world's most important decorative motifs. People painted them on ancient cave walls and glorified them in myths. Flowers have served as an inspiration to poets and painters. Their fragility, fragrance, color, and use in healing have all suggested symbolic meanings for writers and artists.

The publication of botanical books flourished in the late sixteenth century, and by 1600 more than 650 titles had appeared. Famous flower engraver Pierre Joseph Redoute was appointed to Marie Antoinette's cabinet in 1786, and he painted flowers from her garden at the Trianon. After the French Revolution, he worked for Empress Josephine at her estate in Malmaison. Josephine imported unusual plants from around the world, and Redoute was greatly inspired by many of them. In his two famous publications, *Les Roses* (1817 – 1824) and *Les Lilicees* (1802 – 1816), he created some of the most beautiful watercolor paintings of flowers ever made. These publications were used by porcelain artists all over the Continent as subjects for their cabinet plates and dessert services. Of particular beauty are the flowers painted by porcelain artists at Meissen, KPM, and Sevres, and on Royal Copenhagen's Flora Danica dinnerware.

In England, the study of the botanical sciences was greatly enhanced by the establishment of gardens, particularly the Royal Botanic Gardens in Kew founded in 1759. By 1775, Kew had become an important center for the exhibition of exotic plants. Between 1780 and 1810 more than 30 botanical books were published in England, usually illustrated with colored images of flowers and plants. It is not surprising that such a rich source of inspiration should be transferred onto porcelain.

Derby developed the technique of flower painting to its highest form. During 1775 through 1805, Derby sought to attract some of the most famous ceramic artists. Best known was William Billingsly, who became chief flower painter in the 1790s. In the nineteenth century one of the most famous flower artists of all time, Charles Ferdinand Hürten (1820 – 1901), worked for Copeland. Many of his pieces were done for exhibitions, and plates with his signature bring high prices today.

Arrangement of roses, postcard, W2285, printed in Great Britain.

FRUITS

From the beginning, the ancients were enthralled with fruit. Apart from milk and honey, they believed that fruit was nature's only pleasure-laden natural food. Apples, for example, have always been associated with love, beauty, health, comfort, pleasure, sensuality, and fertility. The Latin word *fruor*, meaning "I delight in," is the source of our word *fruit*.

Still life painting, which is the portrayal of a group of inanimate objects, flourished in Europe, particularly Holland, in the seventeenth century. The most common subjects include flowers and fruit. Since fruit was the primary dessert in the eighteenth and nineteenth centuries, it was only natural that porcelain artists depicted fruit on their dessert sets. An extremely rare set of fruit plates was painted by Thomas Baxter at Coalport around 1808 or 1809. The plates are displayed at the Victoria and Albert Museum and are valued at $4,000.00 to $6,000.00 a pair.

To Wish You a Happy Birthday.

Basket of strawberries, postcard, Series #1010, International Art Publishing Co., NY, Berlin.

BIRDS

Pair of birds with nest of babies, postcard.

Through the ages, birds have amused and enchanted their owners with their intelligence, colors, and beautiful songs. Birds have been kept as pets for at least 4,000 years. They are depicted on Egyptian hieroglyphics, which include doves and parrots. The dove is the universal symbol of peace. In the Bible, Noah is said to have sent a dove from his ark to find dry land.

For more than 2,000 years, the mynah bird has been considered sacred in India. It must have been amazing to see individual birds pulled through the cities on oxen during feast days. In ancient Greece, mynahs and parakeets were kept as pets among the aristocracy. The Alexandrine parakeet is named for Alexander the Great.

In wealthy Roman households, one slave had the responsibility of caring for the family bird, which was often a type of parrot. Apparently, watching the parrot talk and perform was the early equivalent of watching TV.

In Europe, the white stork has long been a symbol of good luck. According to legend, the stork delivers newborn babies to homes.

In 1493, Christopher Columbus returned from the New World bearing a pair of Cuban Amazon parrots as a gift to Queen Isabella of Spain.

In the fifteenth century, canaries were trained to accompany miners underground to detect poisonous gases in the shafts. If a canary passed out, the miners knew to get out fast. After the poison-gas terrorist attack in the Japanese subway in 1995, canaries were used for the same purpose.

Pair of peacocks, Swiss postcard #1307.

In 1782, the bald eagle was adopted as the national emblem of the United States. It was chosen because it is such a powerful, noble-looking bird.

Birds have long appealed to Chinese and Japanese potters. A favorite mythological bird which appeared frequently on Chinese ceramics was the elegant ho ho bird, or phoenix, which was the symbol of happiness. It has the head of a pheasant, the tail of a peacock, and the legs of a stork or crane and symbolizes beauty, rank, and longevity.

White cranes in flight are often the subjects painted on Chinese Export items, Japanese Satsuma, Kutani, and Banko ware. The crane means good luck and longevity. In Japan, peacocks stand for elegance and good fortune and are often found together in designs with the peony flower.

From the beginning, the bird was an extremely popular subject at the Meissen manufactory. At the request of the Saxon court, one of the earliest classical tableware designs was decorated with nicely painted native birds. Towards the end of the eighteenth century, bird designs were increasingly in demand for dinner and dessert services. The public showed a preference for colorfully, naturalistically painted birds above all other motifs. Bird studies on porcelain are still popular today. At Royal Worcester, Charles Baldwyn was a popular bird artist specializing in swans.

LANDSCAPES

The word landscape is from the Dutch word *landschap*, a contraction of the word *land* ("land," "area") and the word *scheppen* ("to create"), and means, literally, "created land." The word first appeared in English in the seventeenth century to describe a painted view of land.

Landscape art portrays scenery such as rivers, lakes, mountains, forests, and gardens. The sky is almost always included in the portrait, and weather plays a role in the art as well. First-century Roman frescoes of landscapes are seen on the walls of rooms that have been preserved at Pompeii. In the fifteenth century, landscapes were established in Europe as settings for human activity. Throughout the seventeenth century, landscapes primarily served as settings for important human dramas or animal studies.

At Meissen in the 1730s, porcelain artists experimented with painting European landscapes, based on Dutch engravings, on tea sets, and plates. Soon the paintings of landscapes, battles, and harbor scenes achieved great popularity. River or port scenes, with ships docked along the banks and merchants peddling their wares, are referred to as harbor scenes. They are tiny paintings with deep perspective. Soon other porcelain manufacturers produced landscape scenes.

Lowestoft plate with local views, postcard, British Museum, C. 42.

Porcelain artists began to transfer the paintings in the famous Semper Gallery in Dresden, Germany, onto porcelain around 1800. Giovanni Antonio Canaletto (1697 – 1768) was an Italian painter known for his sparkling views of Venice, Dresden, and other cities in Europe and England. Artists copied his topographical paintings on porcelain, and these items with city views are highly desirable today.

Plate with hand-painted landscape scene, postcard, Davison Bros., London & NY, Series 1414X.

ALLEGORICAL

Tales from Greek and Roman mythology were widely known in the eighteenth century. Famous canvas artists such as Angelica Kaufmann (1741 – 1807) painted pictures in the classical style and inspired porcelain artists. There were abundant classical statues in the gardens and parks of most European and English cities.

WATTEAU COURTING SCENES

Watteau paintings portray figures, usually a man and woman, in a landscape or garden setting. These decorations were copied from originals by eighteenth-century French artists such as François Boucher, Johannes Ridinger, Philips Wouvermen, and Antoine Watteau.

Jean Antoine Watteau (1684 – 1721) was a French rococo artist whose charming graceful paintings show his interest in the theater and ballet. He is best known for his fetes gallante, which are small romantic landscapes with wistful lovers in fancy dress. Watteau scenes were popular subjects at Meissen and KPM and were used extensively by the Dresden decorators, particularly Helena Wolfsohn and Richard Klemm.

Courting scene, postcard.

PORTRAITS

The definition of portrait in *Merriam-Webster's New Collegiate Dictionary*, 11th edition, is "a pictorial representation (as a painting) of a person usu. showing the face." Painters in ancient Rome produced portrait head busts and coins with likenesses of emperors and other famous heroes. They also produced lifelike portraits, as seen in wall paintings from Pompeii.

Over the next 1,000 years, artists incorporated their patrons' full-length portraits into religious paintings. By the fourteenth century, the patrons' facial features, which had been depicted in profile and with little perspective or depth, became more individually correct and recognizable.

Jan van Eyck (1390 – 1441) was one of the best-known Flemish portrait painters. His influence spread throughout Europe. In the 1530s, large portrait chargers were made in Deruta, Italy. A charger of this kind was known as a quartier and had a central medallion of a well-drawn portrait of a lady. The border was made up of four separate decorative panels.

Most of the porcelain artists copied their portraits from earlier well-known oil-on-canvas works by such famous artists as Thomas Gainsborough, Anthony van Dyck, Angelica Kaufmann, Elisabeth Vigee Le Brun, and Joseph Karl Stieler.

Influential Canvas Portrait Artists

Joseph Karl Stieler (1781 – 1858) was the favorite portrait artist of King Ludwig I of Bavaria. The king had a picture gallery in Munich, Germany, devoted to beautiful and chaste women in his kingdom. He selected the women, and as a reward for their cooperation they received the dresses they wore in the paintings. Stieler painted 36 women for Ludwig's gallery from 1827 to 1842. Many of these paintings were reproduced on high-quality Vienna-style and Dresden porcelain plates.

Elisabeth Vigee Le Brun (1755 – 1842) was born in Paris, France. Her father was a respected portrait artist, her mother a peasant hairdresser. Neither had much time for her, and she was sent off to relatives in the country until the age of five, when she returned to Paris and began to take drawing lessons from her father.

From as early as she could remember, Le Brun drew little heads and profiles in the margins of her copybooks. She covered the walls of her dormitory at school with drawings and got in trouble with the nuns. At age 13 her father died, and she had to support her mother and younger brother. She was able to make her living by painting portraits, and she quickly established a following.

In 1774 she exhibited at the Salon of the Academy of St. Luke and was accepted for membership. From that date she became a fashionable portrait painter and began to receive commissions from nobility. Her most impor-

tant client and good friend was Marie Antoinette, and she painted over 30 portraits of her.

Le Brun was an intelligent, talented, and fun-loving woman who enjoyed life and the people she painted. She herself was among the most beautiful French women of the time. It is through her eyes that we see the gaiety and elegance of the French upper classes before the fall of the Bastille in 1789.

It was primarily as a painter of women that she gained her reputation. She not only caught excellent likenesses, but created flattering portrayals as well. In her memoirs, she advised, "Engage them in conversation. Flatter them; tell them they are beautiful; their complexions are marvelous, and they pose well. This put them in good humor."

Le Brun's painting appear in many museums all over the world. She completed over 900 paintings, including 700 portraits. Many Royal Vienna–style and Dresden artists used Le Brun's women as subjects for their portrait plates.

Portrait of Mme. E. L. Vigee Le Brun and her daughter, postcard, Louvre Museum, #521.

Marie Antoinette and her children, painted by E. Vigee Le Brun, Chateau de Versailles, postcard, Eliocromia Zacchetti, Milano.

Angelica Kaufmann (1741 – 1807) was an artist who painted pictures in the classical style. Born in Switzerland, she was recognized as a painter in Rome and then moved to England. There she stayed 15 years, painting portraits

and historical and allegorical pictures. It is said that she married a servant in the belief that he was a count. After giving him a financial settlement, she had the marriage annulled.

Many of Kaufman's paintings were later reproduced on quantities of chinaware in varying degrees of quality. Many decals showing her artwork were produced and were used on plates and other decorative items by ceramic manufacturers in Germany and Austria from around 1870 to the 1920s.

Portrait of the Vestal Virgin, Kauffmann, postcard published by Illustrated Postoral Card Co., NY, Dresden.

Angelo Asti (1807 – 1903) was of Italian ancestry but born in France. He was a well-known painter who exhibited at the Paris salons. Among his works are Art Nouveau style beautiful women. After his death in 1904, some of his portraits were chosen to decorate a calendar, and it was very successful. Asti's women appeared on high-quality color-printed postcards and were reproduced on plates by the Vienna and Dresden decorators.

Portrait of beautiful woman, A. Asti, postcard.

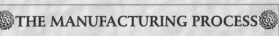

THE MANUFACTURING PROCESS

A DEFINITION OF PORCELAIN

Porcelain is the name originally given to the Chinese ware brought to Europe by the Portuguese and Italian traders returning home with treasures from the Far East. For centuries, porcelain making was a secret known only to the Chinese. When Marco Polo, the Venetian explorer, returned home from the court of Kublai Khan in the thirteenth century, he named the rare pieces of china he brought home with him porcelana, because the glassy surface and texture reminded him of a seashell he knew, a cowrie, called "porcelli" in Italian. Porcelain is the finest textured of all ceramics, which include earthenware, faience, majolica, and stoneware. It is the ultimate in ceramic quality and beauty.

THE INGREDIENTS

There are two kinds of porcelain: Soft paste and hard paste. Soft-paste porcelain differs from hard, or true, porcelain in that it contains large amounts of ground glass, which enables it to be fired at much lower temperatures. Soft-paste porcelain is vitreous and translucent.

True, or hard-paste porcelain, is composed principally of feldspar, quartz, and kaolin, which produce a fine clay that is virtually free of impurities. The relative amounts of these three ingredients vary according to the texture that is desired. The more kaolin, the harder the porcelain. Fired at very high temperatures, hard-paste porcelain is characteristically translucent and white and has great strength and hardness. It is almost always cast in molds. The beauty and decorative potential of the pure white clay more than compensates for the technical problems involved in its production. As the process and materials for hard-paste porcelain became better understood, the making of soft paste porcelain was gradually phased out.

The ingredients of porcelain are carefully washed,

ground, and pulverized before they are mixed together. Water is then pressed out of the creamy liquid, and this results in a workable clay which can be stored until it is needed.

PREPARATION

There are two basic methods of taking a shapeless lump of clay and making it into an object of beauty and usefulness such as a decorative plate. Throwing is one method, and molding is another.

The throwing method is certainly not for mass producing an item, but it has a kind of charm. In the throwing method, a portion of clay is centered on the potter's wheel, and as it rotates, the potter skillfully shapes it with his hands to the desired form. It has that one-of-a-kind personal touch that is not possible from mass production.

Molding is ideal for long production runs of objects which have to be identical in form and size, and for intricate shapes. When cakes of clay paste are in a workable state, they are ready for one of three methods of molding: jiggering, jollying, or casting.

After any one of the three processes is completed, the piece is trimmed and sponged to a smooth finish.

Casting workshop, Sevres, postcard.

If assembly of the pieces is required — for instance, if handles need to be attached to a cake plate — this is accomplished by using slip to attach the additional piece or pieces to the form.

Manufacturing workshop, Sevres, postcard.

DESIGNING AND MODELING

To create a new shape, a designer must first draw each item and establish a design. A model must then be made before a piece of fine porcelain can be produced. The modeler must bear in mind that there will be a reduction in size during the bisque firing, so the model must be at least six percent larger that the finished item. The model is usually made of plaster of Paris or a resin material.

Plates are actually produced from working molds. These molds are exact copies in the reverse of the original model. Molds must be very dry before they are used, so that the dry plaster wall will quickly absorb moisture from the paste. To produce a single item in large quantities,

Manufacturing workshop, Sevres, postcard.

many working molds may be required, as the molds wear out. In a plate, a working mold is required for the shape of the plate itself. Slip is used as an adhesive to add any external decoration. Making these separate working molds is a true art requiring great skill. Model and mold making are two of the most important parts of the production process.

Manufacturing workshop, Sevres, postcard.

BISQUE FIRING

The first firing of a piece is called bisque, or biscuit, and the piece requires very careful handling. The molded piece goes into a kiln. It takes a piece about 30 hours of firing, and the piece will reach temperatures as high as 1,750 degrees Fahrenheit. After cooling to room temperature, it is ready for further processing.

Putting plates into kilns, Sevres, postcard.

F. F.
PARIS
52405. - MANUFACTURE de SEVRES. - Un Four

149. **Manufacture Nationale de Porcelaine de Sèvres** F. F.
Atelier de Ciselure
PARIS

GLAZE

The glaze applied to a plate serves several purposes. The first is to form a completely impenetrable surface; the second, to provide durability to the items for long and hard usage; and last, to produce the translucency which is characteristic of fine porcelain plates.

Quartz, feldspar, chalk, and dolomite are mixed together to make a creamy liquid called glaze. The

ingredients may vary slightly from company to company for the desired effect.

Glaze is applied to a plate by dipping the piece in a vat of the liquid. The bisque piece is very absorbent, and a layer of glaze is built up. The glaze must be of just the right thickness.

LAST FIRING

After being glazed, a plate is put in a kiln for a second firing, which is done at about 2100°F. More firings may be required, depending on the quality and degree of painting and gilding desired.

FINAL TOUCHES

After the final firing, some plates may be lined. Lining is accomplished when a plate is placed on a spinning platform and an artist uses a brush to apply decoration to the rim of the plate. This decoration is usually gold, silver, or enamels. A decal can also be put in place at this time.

Porcelain may be decorated at a number of stages in its production. Prior to glazing, the bisque ware is often decorated with colored underglazes or stains. The glaze is applied to the bisque and fired at a much lower temperature than the clay body itself. After the ware has been glazed and fired, it is often further decorated with overglaze enamels, metallic lusters, or decals and then fired yet again at an even lower temperature.

The final step of the manufacturing process is the inspection. To be acceptable, a plate must be free of any defects. Although there are inspections along the way, it's very important that a final inspection is completed. When all the processes have been completed, with some minor variations depending on the specific manufacturer, we have a beautiful finished plate ready for decoration. It takes a group of many talented, skilled people working together to produce a plate.

Girl painting a plate, Royal Delftware Factory, de Porceleyne Fles.

AMERICAN PLATES

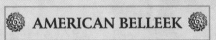

AMERICAN BELLEEK

In the United States, cabinet plates in American Belleek are of exceptional quality and are sure to please the most discriminating collector. From 1883 until 1920, several potteries located in New Jersey and Ohio manufactured a type of china similar to the famous Irish Belleek parian. This luxury china is considered the highest achievement of the American porcelain industry.

CAC/LENOX

In the mid-nineteenth century, it was impossible to find American china fine enough to decorate the home. Although potteries had sprung up all over the United States, they produced utilitarian wares almost exclusively. Buyers looked to Europe for their fine porcelain, and some American pottery companies began stamping their wares with French-sounding names in order to sell them.

Then along came a man with a dream. A man who had a vision of producing a porcelain as fine as any made in the world. This visionary was Walter Scott Lenox.

As young Walter Scott Lenox walked home from school in Trenton, New Jersey, in the 1870s, he would stop by one of the many ceramics companies and watch the potter at his wheel. It must have been magical to the young would-be artist to see a lump of clay being turned into a useful object such as a pitcher or plate. Lenox realized he had to learn the basics of the trade before becoming a designer and offered his services free for a year to a company run by Isaac Davis. At the end of the

year, Davis was so pleased with his work that he offered Lenox a large salary to continue.

After a few years spent learning the trade, Lenox became art director for Ott & Brewer (1881 – 1884) and Willets Manufacturing Company (1884 – 1889), where he was instrumental in the development of American Belleek in Trenton. Delicate Belleek porcelain with its unique pearl-luster glaze and thin, translucent body was first produced by the David McBirney factory in Belleek, Ireland.

With a small amount of money, Lenox and three partners founded the Ceramic Art Company in May 1889. It was Lenox's dream to produce an American porcelain as fine as any made in the world, and to achieve this new departure in American ceramics, Lenox hired a talented staff of decorators and artists from all over the world. This combination of artistic effort allowed beautiful works of art, including cabinet plates, to be produced that today are valued by collectors.

The early plates were highly ornate with naturalistic themes, such as marine life, birds, flowers, and fruit. They were designed in the Aesthetic style with raised gold and sometimes silver and bronze. Monks, hunting scenes, and beautiful women were also favorite subjects decorating the plates. The company also produced whiteware for amateur decoration.

The firm began making bone china service plates for its affluent customers, such as private clubs, hotels, and wealthy families in 1902. This was continued for several decades, and one of the artists, William Morley, was considered one of the finest china painters in the world. His best-known subject was orchids. He also painted sets of plates with snow birds, fish, and fruit.

In 1906 the name Ceramic Art Company was changed to Lenox, Inc., to reflect Walter Scott's sole ownership of the firm, and the marks changed to show the new name. Frank Grahams Holmes's arrival marked a new beginning for Lenox. He decided to make tableware out of its distinctive ivory Belleek, as well as bone china, using contemporary designs.

The next major development was in 1917, when the first lithographed pattern, Ming, was introduced. With this decal decoration, Lenox could offer high-quality tableware to a larger audience at lower prices. When the Tiffany Company took an interest in Lenox's dinnerware and displayed it in its showrooms in New York and Philadelphia, the wealthy customers accepted it as the best money could buy.

The Lenox Company had a landmark year in 1918. President Woodrow Wilson decided to select an American-made china for use in the White House and, for the first time in history, commissioned a 1,700-piece dinnerware service from an American company, Lenox, at a cost of $11,251.00. Designed by Holmes, the china had a pure white center and an outer and inner border of 24kt gold, enclosing an ivory rim having the seal of the United States. With this exciting commission a new period was begun, and soon the entire factory was devoted to tableware.

COLUMBIA ART POTTERY

The Columbia Art Pottery was in existence from 1893 to 1902 in Trenton, New Jersey. It was established by W. T. Morris and F. R. Willmore, hence the initials *M* and *W* in the shield or bell trademark. Both men came from England and worked at the Royal Worcester pottery before coming to the United States. Morris also worked for the Irish Belleek factory. When they landed in Trenton, they worked for a short period at Ott & Brewer before deciding to work for themselves. They started the Columbia Art Pottery (CAP) in 1893 in Trenton, New Jersey. The CAP was named for the Columbian Exposition held in Chicago in 1893. The company made vases, ewers, plates, and souvenir pieces decorated in the Worcester style. Most of its pieces were made with a Belleek body, and plates can be found decorated with heavy paste flowers and leaves on a cream ground. The company was open for just nine years and closed in 1902.

OTT & BREWER

The first company to make American Belleek was Ott

& Brewer. The company was founded in 1863 by William Bloor and was first known as Bloor, Ott & Brewer. It was located in Trenton, New Jersey. About that time, the city of Trenton began to establish itself as a premier pottery production center. China clay deposits were found in the area, and it had a geographical advantage because of its location between New York City and Philadelphia. The railroad could bring coal from Pennsylvania to fuel the kilns and between the railroad and waterway provided ways of shipping the finish goods. Trenton, New Jersey, became known as the Staffordshire of America.

In 1871 the company was renamed Ott & Brewer. John Hart Brewer was the artistic director. At this time, the company employed Isaac Broome, an outstanding nineteenth-century American ceramic sculptor, to produce a line of parianware for the American Centennial in 1876. Broome's works at Ott & Brewer are among the most famous ceramic pieces ever produced in this country.

Ott & Brewer created some exceptional cabinet plates and pioneered the introduction and development of Belleek in the United States. Many of Ott & Brewer's workers went on to produce art porcelain at other potteries.

WILLETS MANUFACTURING

The Willets Manufacturing Company operated in Trenton, New Jersey, from around 1879 to 1909. The company made a wide variety of items, including cabinet plates. In 1884, Walter Scott Lenox became head of the decorating department and began making hard-paste porcelain. William Bromley, Sr., came to Willets in 1887 and brought his formula for Belleek porcelains. The Belleek items were exquisite and delicate and are eagerly collected today. An example is a set of plates painted by E. M. Giltons. They are beautifully hand painted with different types of fruit. The Willets Company continued production until 1909.

THE DECLINE OF THE TRENTON POTTERY INDUSTRY

There are several factors that led to the decline of the art porcelain business in Trenton, New Jersey. First was a workers' strike in 1894, which lasted for six long months, and another in 1895. These strikes caused increased costs for the companies. The start of World War I took a toll on the available labor. Other factors which helped with the demise of the ceramic industry in Trenton were the increased use of plastics and the resistance of workers to new methods of production. Two other factors were a lawsuit by the Irish Belleek company prohibiting the Trenton companies from using the name Belleek, and of course, the Great Depression. Today only Lenox has survived.

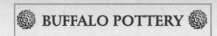
The Buffalo Pottery Company was founded by Larkin Soap in 1903 in order to produce wares to be used as premiums given away with the soap. It was the dream of three of the top executives of Buffalo Pottery, Louis Brown, William Rea, and Ralph Stuart, to produce a fine art-pottery line that could compete with the popular English Staffordshire potteries.

The result was the Deldare line, produced in 1908 and 1909 and again from 1923 to 1925. It has a distinctive olive green body overlaid with colorful figures and scenes of English life. Many of the scenes were reproduced from drawings by the famous English watercolorist Cecil Alden. The ware has elaborate transfer decorations that were painstakingly hand colored. Each piece was initialed by the artist. Deldare was a popular pattern, but quite labor-intensive and expensive to make.

In 1911 a completely different type of ware, called Emerald Ware, was produced for just one year, and it is now one of the most highly prized of all Buffalo china types. Another art line followed that was called Albino Ware. It was the same as Deldare, but the colors were painted softer, in rust and pale green.

Buffalo Pottery is still active as a china producer today; it is part of the Oneida Company. It is one of the largest U.S. producers of hotel and institutional ware.

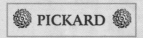
PICKARD

Pickard, Inc., was established by Wilder Pickard in Edgerton, Wisconsin, in 1894 as a decorating firm. The company bought porcelain blanks, mainly from European firms, such as those in Limoges, and decorated the pieces with fruits, floral, birds, portraits, and scenes with gold embellishments. Pickard's ambition was to raise china decoration to the quality of fine art.

Early designs were colorful and naturalistic, resembling European porcelain of the period. Soon porcelain artists developed stylized designs, such as Conventional, which reflected the Art Nouveau movement. Another popular stylized pattern was Aura Argenta Linear.

Gold-encrusted and gold-etched porcelains were introduced in 1911 and became Pickard's most popular lines. In 1912, Pickard introduced a very successful line called Vellum. One of the artists who developed the Vellum landscape scenes was Edward Stafford Challinor. The colors were applied in delicate pastels with a matt finish. Another artist, Curtis Marker, was also instrumental in the development of the Vellum style of painting.

In 1938 Pickard starting making its own porcelain. Since 1976, it has issued an annual limited-edition Christmas plate. Pickard, Inc., is still in business today and is presently located in Antioch, Illinois.

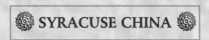
SYRACUSE CHINA

The Onondaga Pottery Company began operation in Syracuse, New York, in 1871. By 1890, it was making a vitrified china that was white, translucent, and stronger than European porcelain. In 1893, "Syracuse China" was introduced and awarded a medal at the Colombian Exposition in Chicago. In 1896, the company created its "rolled edge" china, which became a standard body form. Syracuse China discontinued its line of china for home use in 1970. In 1971, it became one of the country's largest producers of hotel, restaurant, airline, and other commercial tableware.

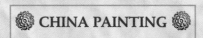
CHINA PAINTING

The development of china painting as an art form in the United States is said to have had its roots in the Arts and Crafts movement of the late nineteenth century. Instead of relying on foreign goods, Americans became interested in their own arts and crafts.

Another important factor was the increasingly active role in the arts which American women were embracing. China painting, a delicate and relatively neat and clean art, held great appeal for women. Middle-class women could engage in it without compromising their husbands' social standings. It was also an occupation in which women from lower incomes could engage

rather than going into sweatshop environments. For both classes of women, it offered an opportunity for creative expression.

By 1905, it was estimated that there were some 20,000 professional china decorators. We have not heard about home parties, but we are sure they were a common occurrence during the heyday of the china painting craze. Much of the porcelain whiteware used by these artists was imported from European manufacturers, such as those in Limoges, France. Plates that are home decorated are often quite beautiful and unique, and they should be judged on their individual merits.

Columbian Art Co., Trenton, c. 1893 – 1902. Belleek plate, 9½"; pink flowers with raised gold ferns center, yellow border. $350.00 – 375.00. (See mark #21.)

Deldare, c. 1908, artist signed "L. Newman." Chop plate, 14"; An Evening at Ye Lion Inn. $600.00 – 700.00.

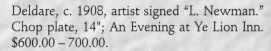

Lenox, c. 1906 – 1930, made for Tiffany & Co, artist signed "W. Morley." 9"; etched gold border, hand-painted snow birds. $100.00 – 125.00. (See mark #62.)

Lenox, c. 1906 – 1930, made for Tiffany & Co, artist signed "W. Morley." 9"; etched gold border, hand-painted snow birds. $100.00 – 125.00.

Lenox, c. 1906 – 1930, made for Tiffany & Co. Service plate, 10¹/₃"; garlands of enameled flowers, etched gold border. $75.00 – 100.00.

Lenox, c. 1906 – 1930. 9¹/₄"; gilt and green border. $50.00 – 75.00.

Pickard, c. 1930 – 1938, Heinrich & Co. blank. Service plate, 10³/₄", floral transfer in center, gilt decoration on border. $50.00 – 75.00. (See mark #121.)

Pickard type, unmarked, c. 1914 – 1915, artist signed "A. Leigh." Charger, 13"; hand-painted water lilies with gold border, artist worked for Pickard. $150.00 – 200.00.

Pickard, c. 1925 – 1930, artist signed "Marker." Two-handled Vellum cake plate, 11¼"; landscape scene, 1¾" etched gold border. $400.00 – 500.00.

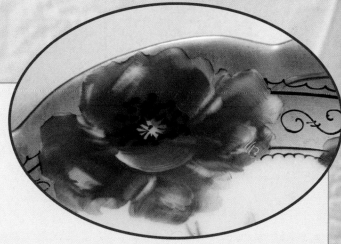

Close-up poppy.

Pickard, c. 1925 – 1930, artist signed "E. N." 8½"; Art Nouveau with five stylized poppies with aqua and green leaves, gold border. $250.00 – 300.00. (See mark #122.)

Pickard, c. 1912 – 1918, artist signed "Marker." Cake plate one handle, 9¼"; landscape scene, Vellum. $300.00 – 400.00. (See mark #123.)

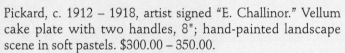

Pickard, c. 1912 – 1918, artist signed "E. Challinor." Vellum cake plate with two handles, 8"; hand-painted landscape scene in soft pastels. $300.00 – 350.00.

Pickard, c. 1903 – 1905, Haviland blank, attributed to Joseph Blaha. 7¾"; hand-painted red cherries. $200.00 – 250.00.

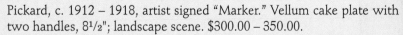

Pickard, c. 1912 – 1918, artist signed "Marker." Vellum cake plate with two handles, 8½"; landscape scene. $300.00 – 350.00.

Pickard, c. 1928 – 1938, Hutschenreuther blank. Service plate, 10½"; lavish decoration. $75.00 – 100.00. (See mark #124.)

Pickard, c. 1905 – 1910, artist signed "Nathan Gifford." 8¾"; Art Nouveau style with strawberries, gooseberries, and cherry blossoms. $250.00 – 300.00.

Pickard, c. 1919 – 1922, artist signed "E. Challinor." Two-handled cake plate, 10½"; Peacock pattern. $500.00 – 550.00. (See mark #125.)

Close-up of peacock.

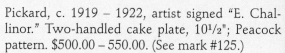

Syracuse China, c. 1970s. 4¹/₂"; boxer transfer designed by Stuart Bruce. $25.00 – 30.00. (See mark #143.)

Taylor, Smith & Taylor, c. 1930 – 1960s. Semi-porcelain platter, 14"; Reveille pattern. $35.00 – 40.00.

Vernon Kilns, California, c. 1945 – 1958. Charger, 12¹/₄"; Brown Eyed Susan pattern, hand painted. $40.00 – 45.00.

Wheeling Pottery Co., Wheeling, WV, c. 1893 – 1900, La Belle China mark. Flow Blue, 10"; floral design. $100.00 – 125.00. (See mark #158.)

Willets Manufacturing, c. 1880 – 1904. Scalloped Belleek, 8¹/₂"; hand-painted rose with purple lilacs in the foreground, gold on border. $150.00 – 175.00. (See mark #159.)

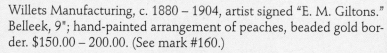

Willets Manufacturing, c. 1880 – 1904, artist signed "E. M. Giltons." Belleek, 9"; hand-painted arrangement of peaches, beaded gold border. $150.00 – 200.00. (See mark #160.)

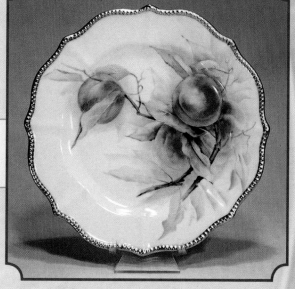

Willets Manufacturing, c. 1880 – 1904, artist signed "E. M. Giltons." Belleek, 9"; hand-painted arrangement of plums, beaded gold border. $150.00 – 200.00.

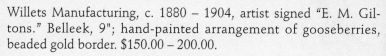

Willets Manufacturing, c. 1880 – 1904, artist signed "E. M. Giltons." Belleek, 9"; hand-painted arrangement of gooseberries, beaded gold border. $150.00 – 200.00.

Willets Manufacturing, c. 1880 – 1904, artist signed "E. M. Giltons." Belleek, 9"; hand-painted arrangement of cherries, beaded gold border. $150.00 – 200.00.

Close-up cherries.

Willets Manufacturing, c. 1880 – 1904, artist signed "S. M. Gonzales." 9¹/₈"; colorful hand-painted wood ducks, etched gold on border. $250.00 – 300.00.

Willets Manufacturing, c. 1880 – 1904. Scalloped, 8¹/₂"; hand-painted pastel flowers, gilt leaves. $200.00 – 250.00.

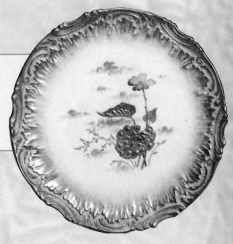

Unidentified sunburst mark, c. 1880 – 1900. Reticulated, majolica, 7"; floral and fern pattern. $100.00 – 125.00.

Majolica, unidentified maker, c. 1890s. Oak leaf–shaped bread tray, 12"; greens and yellows with acorn. $100.00 – 125.00.

Majolica, unidentified maker, c. 1890s. Bread tray, 14"; bird and flowering branch. $250.00 – 300.00.

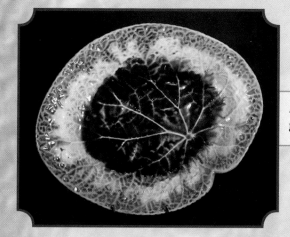

Majolica, unidentified maker, c. 1890s. Leaf-shaped dish, 7¼"; green and brown leaf decoration. $100.00 – 125.00.

Limoges, Bawo & Dotter, c. 1900. 9¼"; Art Nouveau style, home decorated, portrait of lady with flowing hair and garland of grapes around her head on a gold medallion, green matte background with grapes. $350.00 – 500.00.

Limoges, T & V, artist signed and dated 1912. Charger, 12½"; home decorated, hand-painted ears of corn on shades of green. $150.00 – 200.00.

Limoges, Charles Martin, c. 1891, artist signed "E. Hemm." Charger, 13¾"; home decorated, hand-painted colorful poppies. $300.00 – 350.00. (See mark #70.)

Limoges, Charles Martin, c. 1891+. Charger, 12½"; hand-painted mums in pink and white, home decorated, pierced for hanging. $150.00 – 250.00.

Limoges, Lanternier, c. 1891 – 1914. 9¾"; amateur decorated, portrait of St. Bernard dog. $75.00 – 100.00. (See mark #84.)

STAFFORDSHIRE TRANSFERWARE PLATES

Some of the most eagerly collected plates are the Staffordshire blue and white scenic plates from England. Staffordshire is not a company, but a geographical area encompassing 12 shires in England. Many English potters established themselves in the Staffordshire region because the clays were superior to those from any other area in England. Pottery has been made in the district since the days of the Romans.

In the late eighteenth century, there were as many as 80 different manufacturers in the Staffordshire district. By 1802, the number had increased to 149. No single company is responsible for manufacturing Staffordshire plates. It was a group effort, and each potter used a different border to express individuality. The border could have scrolls, lace, flowers, medallions, shells, or trees. Back stamps often indicated the pattern with or without the maker's trademark. Several companies used the same patterns, and identifying some plates can be confusing.

TRANSFER PRINTING

Staffordshire plates were made of earthenware pottery and were decorated by a method called transfer printing, which was developed around 1755. This inexpensive method of decoration was accomplished by engraving a design onto a copper plate which was then inked and applied to thin paper. The paper was pressed to the plate, leaving some ink behind. The piece was then glazed.

SUBJECTS

"Among true antiques commemorating our nation's beginning are the historical plates known as Historical Staffordshire, occasionally referred to as talking plates because of the scenes depicted upon their face."
(Bane, Reynolds. "Historical Plates of Staffordshire."
The Antique Trader Anthology V, 1976)

Scenic views of the Orient and of romantic European destinations with castles and towns became popular. The most valuable plates, however, are those with American scenes produced between 1800 and 1848. Enterprising English potters arranged to have artists traveling in America sketch the sites for their wares. Leading Staffordshire potters like Adams, Clews, Davenport, Meigh, Ridgway, Stevens and Wood, and hundreds of small companies made American views.

COLORS

Deep cobalt blue and white designs were among the earliest made, and these remain sentimental favorites in the United States and England. As technology expanded, the shade lightened. By 1850 other colors were being used, such as pink, red, black, green, brown, and purple.

FLOW BLUE

The Flow Blue process was discovered in England in the late eighteenth century as a result of combining cobalt blue underglaze decoration and transfer printing. The process occurs when a volatizing agent such as ammonia or lime of chloride is added, causing the pattern to "bleed" during the glaze firing stage. This romantic flowing characteristic captured the imagination of the English and American markets.

The earliest patterns were Oriental in style, with scenics and florals being most popular. Over 1,500 patterns were manufactured during the peak years of Flow Blue production from the mid-1800s to the early 1900s.

WEDGWOOD HISTORICAL PLATES

At the end of the nineteenth century, Wedgwood made a number of blue and white historical plates with many views of America. They were imported by the Boston importer Jones, McDuffee & Stratton Company. The plates copied the old Staffordshire wares which were made from around 1820 to 1850.

The original 35 different landscapes were copyrighted in 1899. They were all done in a deep blue and white transfer print. The series was tied together with a common floral border. The center of each plate had a view of an American landscape or historical event, and the scenes were mainly set in New England, particularly Boston. The plate had the title on the reverse as well as some historical information. Each plate had the Wedgwood and importer logos. The original retail price was 50 cents each. By 1910, the plates were so popular the price was reduced to 35 cents. These sell for about $75.00 – 100.00 today.

Some colleges and universities had Wedgwood plates created for them through the Jones, McDuffee & Stratton Company beginning in 1925. Harvard University was the leader, having four series of 12 different scenes. In the 75 years in which Wedgwood produced plates with landscapes of America for the importer, over 1,000 different views were produced.

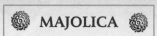

MAJOLICA

Majolica dates from medieval Italy, when it was an everyday pottery glazed with an opaque tin enamel in purples and coppery greens. It was in nineteenth century England that majolica appeared again. Herbert Minton started the craze, calling his brightly colored pottery with heavy relief nature themes "majolica." Then makers from all over England, Europe, and America started to turn out similar whimsical wares. Some plates have interesting naturalistic designs, such as two parrots on a branch, a flying crane and water lily, and fruit and flowers of all types. Some of the most desirable and valuable oyster plates are made of English majolica.

BONE CHINA

Bone china became the standard English porcelain body throughout the nineteenth century and remains the preferred china today. The light weight and translucency of bone china makes it appealing for dessert and dinnerware. Bone china is made using crushed animal bone that is combined with clay, giving the mixture more stability. Some bone china is so fine you can usually see your hand through it when its held up to the light.

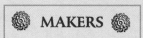

MAKERS

AYNSLEY

John Aynsley established a pottery in 1775 in Longton and produced some beautiful dinner and dessert services. By the turn of the nineteenth century, he was making them of bone china, still the present company's specialty. His aim, carried on today, was to produce a superior type of body, pure in tone but sound and durable, in shapes that were useful and artistic.

Aynsley received royal patronage many times in the twentieth century. Queen Elizabeth selected an Aynsley service at the time of her wedding, as did the late Princess Diana.

Tea and dessert sets were made with floral and scenic decoration. Fruit decoration was also very popular with collectors. Aynsley artists Nancy Brunt and Doris Jones specialized in fruit painting in the 1930s through the 1950s. They were influenced by the fruit decoration created by Royal Worcester.

In 1969 Aynsley joined with Waterford Crystal. Today Aynsley operates four factories within the Stoke-on-Trent area. Aynsley continues to maintain the very highest standards of quality and workmanship.

BODLEY

Quality porcelain was produced by Bodley from 1875 to 1892. Edwin James Drew Bodley worked at Samuel Alcock's Old Hill Pottery at Burslem, which had been divided into separate china and earthenware factories in 1867. The china works (now called Crown Works) was taken over first by Bodley and Diggory and then by Bodley & Son until Edwin J. D. Bodley began to do business under his own name in June 1875. Bodley produced fine quality porcelains in the Aesthetic style. Relief gilt dessert sets with flowers, birds, and butterflies in burnished gold and silver were produced on ivory, pink, yellow, or pale blue grounds.

BOSSONS

W. H. Bossons, Ltd., was founded in 1946 in Congleton, Cheshire, England. William Henry Bossons, who started the company, died in 1951. His son, Ray, who succeeded him, was an accomplished craftsman, and he continued in the same traditions of his father as chairman and managing director of the factory. Both father and son learned their craft at the Burslem School of Art in Stoke-on-Trent, Staffordshire.

When Ray Bossons became ill and was unable to actively continue as the head of the company, his daughter, Jane Roberts, took over the operations. Not having the same interest as her father and having no desire to sell the company, she decided to cease production in December 1996.

The company started out making toy soldiers, but quickly shifted its production to scenic wall plaques, made of plaster of Paris, of famous historical locations all around the English countryside. Ray Bossons was a perfectionist in all phases of the business. After considerable research into the geography or history of the scene he was planning to create, he did all the sketches for the wall plaques himself. The original models were first done in clay by a skilled artist. A case mold was then made by a model maker. From this, a plaster model was produced. A special process picked up the fine details and transferred them to the final product. When the model was completely dried, a staff of artists painted each piece with watercolors. A colorless lacquer was then applied after the paint dried, to give each plaque a matte finish. The Bossons wall plaques have lifelike detail and are eagerly collected today.

WILLIAM BROWNFIELD & SONS

William Brownfield & Sons was in operation in Cobridge, Staffordshire, from 1850 to 1900. The company made a variety of transferware plates and exported many to the United States. In the 1870s, under the direction of Louis Jahn, a former Minton employee, Brownfield began the manufacture of porcelain and majolica. It exhibited its wares at world exhibitions, and some of its hand-painted dessert services bring high prices at auctions today.

CAULDON

Cauldon began operation in 1905 in Hanley, England. It had previously been Brown-Westhead, Moore & Company. Although the firm is best known for its useful wares, it also produced a number of interesting decorative lines. It produced dinnerware and dessert services for firms like Tiffany & Co. and Davis, Collamore & Co. of New York City.

COALPORT

Coalport's history goes back to 1750 when Squire Brown of Caughley Hill in Shropshire began producing pottery using clay and coal from his estate. When he died, his nephew took the business over. He was joined in 1772 by Thomas Turner. The firm was sold in 1799 to John Rose, who had founded a manufactory at Coalport village. In 1926 Coalport moved from Shropshire to Stoke-on-Trent. In 1967 it became a member of the Wedgwood Group.

Coalport cabinet and dessert plates are highly regarded today. During the nineteenth century, popular ground colors were celadon, pink, pale yellow, ivory, turquoise, and cobalt blue. Turquoise was used with a number of patterns based upon Far Eastern designs. The turquoise was sometimes overlaid with gold decoration, including stylized Japanese peonies or raised water lilies. Cobalt blue was often used because of the great richness and depth of color that it suggested.

Some of the most desirable Coalport cabinet plates feature gold and enamel jewels on gold ground. These jewels, or enamel droplets, were applied by hand. In addition to the fine jeweled decoration, some of the rarest of these cabinet pieces also have hand-painted cartouches with landscapes, birds, or flowers.

COPELAND SPODE

Josiah Spode established his factory in 1784 in Stoke. At the end of the eighteenth century, Josiah Spode was responsible for the single most important development in his industry — the perfection of the formula for fine bone china. It was the whitest, most translucent, strongest, and most resonant bone china in the industry.

He also perfected the process of blue underglaze printing, and Spode's blue and white designs have become some of the most sought after in the history of ceramics. The East India Company in Canton, China, the world's largest dealer in porcelain, ordered its own armorial service from Spode in 1823. Three original patterns that are still being produced today are Tower Blue, Willow, and Blue Italian, a collector favorite.

After three generations, William Taylor Copeland bought the firm from Josiah III in 1833. In 1976 Spode became part of the Royal Worcester Company and became known as the Royal Worcester Spode Group. Today Spode tableware is basically still being made the same way, and the original bone china formula is still being used.

During the second half of the nineteenth century, the company created beautiful hand-painted and jeweled porcelain. (Plates were decorated with drops of enamel in relief imitating pearls; this was called jeweling.) The company had a special mark for such decoration. Copeland Spode had a number of talented artists. David Evans painted floral decoration until the middle of the nineteenth century. He was succeeded by German painter Charles Ferdinand Hürten (1820 – 1901), who worked for the factory from 1859 to 1897.

Hürten was born in Germany in 1818 and trained at the Cologne School of Art. He was noted for his exceptional flower painting and began doing commission work for the Sevres factory. He joined Copeland in 1859 after W. T. Copeland had seen his work at the 1855 International Exhibition. He was given his own studio and allowed to paint freely. Hürten was allowed to sign his work, which was unheard of during that time. In an 1862 exhibition, the Royal Family saw his magnificent flower painting and commissioned the famous Prince of Wales dessert set. It was ordered by the Prince for his marriage to Princess Alexandra of Denmark in 1863. The plates were reticulated and jeweled with floral cartouches painted by Hürten.

A highly talented figure painter for Copeland Spode was Samuel Alcock (1845 – 1914). He was so temperamental and self-important that he would not work at the factory, so his work was brought to him at home. Alcock's most famous service was the Midsummer Night's Dream Service which was exhibited in the Paris Exhibition of 1889. Each plate portrayed a different scene from the Shakespearean play. Alcock painted ladies of fashion, Watteau subjects, and Gainsborough heads. His dessert plates often had jeweled borders done by the finest gilders.

ROYAL CROWN DERBY

William Duesbury opened the Derby Works in Derby, England, in 1755. The specialty of Derby was cabinet wares, particular tea and dessert services. Perhaps more than any other English company, Royal Crown Derby was inspired by the Far East for its designs and developed a great number of Imari- and Persian-style patterns. They used rich, jewel-colored grounds of mazarine, cobalt blue, coral, and jade green ornamented with heavily raised chased gold. The designs were inspired by the birds, flowers, insects, and traditional motifs seen on priceless carpets and embroideries.

Their raised gilding was achieved by using a paste made from glass frits, ground enamel color, and a small amount of flux bound together with turpentine. The paste was applied to the hand-drawn designs using a fine sable brush, after which the piece was fired in the kiln.

Royal Crown Derby made many plates purely for display in cabinets, as well as wonderful dessert services. Famous artists were James Platts (figures), James Rouse (flowers), J. Brownswood (flowers), and E. Trowell (landscapes). In addition to the Japanese Imari patterns for which the company is famous, these artists brought the Sevres style up to date with delicate painting on richly colored grounds. Reserve paintings were framed with colored jeweling and the finest raised gold.

CROWN DUCAL

In 1915, Albert Goodwin Richardson bought the Gordon Pottery in Tunistall, England, and renamed it A. G. Richardson, Ltd. His purpose was to produce good-quality earthenware under the name Crown Ducal. In 1919 he sold his interest to Harry Taylor, who owned a lithograph company. The use of chintz transfers expanded rapidly.

The United States was a major importer of Crown Ducal, and it had great appeal for Americans during the late 1920s through the 1950s. Old catalogs show the company's innovative advertising efforts. For example, it introduced the Florida pattern in 1925 as "a wordless song of the tropics."

A deep ivory glaze base color was developed at Richardson's in 1931, and a number of chintz patterns had it. The company was acquired by the Wedgwood Group in 1980 and renamed Unicorn Pottery. Popular patterns are Blue Chintz, Purple Chintz, and Florida.

ROYAL DOULTON

The production of rack plates by Doulton goes back to the earliest days of the pottery at Lambeth. Plates were made of salt-glazed stoneware. The Doulton pottery at Burslem produced a large number of transfer rack plates. The Gibson Girl series was produced around 1902 and was extremely popular with collectors.

Head, or portrait, plates formed one of the most important categories of Doulton rack plates. A Charles Dickens plate was made in 1911. It has the head of Dickens in the center of the plate surrounded by a border of characters from Dickens's novels. Plates were also produced of Shakespeare and Robert Burns. A series of scenic rack plates includes Tower of London, Anne Hathaway's College, Edinburgh Castle, and many more.

The Doulton factory at Burslem produced some beautifully decorated cabinet plates and dessert services, as well as several series of hand-painted game plates. Famous artists included Percy Curock, Daniel Dewsbury, Edward Raby, and Charles Noke. Flowers were a very popular subject, usually done in muted colors outlined in gold.

HAMMERSLEY

The first potter associated with this manufactory is probably George Harris Hammersley, who worked with a partner, Harvey Adams, in 1885. The company became Hammersley & Co. in 1887. The company produced

many lovely dessert and dinnerware sets. An exceptional dessert set hand-painted by F. A. Marple portrays beautifully painted birds in scenic settings. The company is part of the Royal Worcester Spode Ltd. Group today.

IRISH BELLEEK

David McBirney and Robert Armstrong founded the Belleek Pottery Company in County Fermanagh, Ireland, in 1857. Using local clay deposits, they soon produced Belleek parian china, which was extremely thin and light with a creamy ivory surface and pearl-like luster. Today the dinnerware is still hand crafted, just as it was more than 100 years ago. Shamrock, Tridacna, Neptune, and Mask are but a few of the eagerly collected patterns, the Shamrock being the most popular.

To many collectors, the examples of Belleek's woven baskets, trays, and cake plates represent the epitome of the pottery's production. All the latticework is woven by hand, as is the wonderful applied flower decoration.

JOHNSON BROTHERS

Four Johnson brothers took over the Charles Street Works Pottery in Staffordshire, England, in 1883. They made tablewares that were successful in England and in the United States. Their wares were originally earthenware and white ironstone. In 1885, the whiteware was replaced by a lighter-weight ware known for its lightness and finer finish. It is this quality ironstone which has been the mainstay of the Johnson Brothers tableware business. In 1968, the company became part of the Wedgwood Group.

GEORGE JONES

The George Jones & Sons pottery was established in 1861 with the production of white granite ware, and in 1865 manufactured earthenware. Majolica production started around 1866. In 1876, fine bone china was first produced.

At the start of the twentieth century, George Jones & Sons, Ltd., was the third largest pottery manufacturer in England. It employed 1,000 workers and exported at least half of its production. The company was in operation for some 100 years, starting in 1861. It closed its doors in 1951.

What set George Jones apart from some of the other porcelain manufacturers in Stoke-on-Trent was its emphasis on decoration. Hand painting became the company's specialty in the mid-nineteenth century, and many talented artists joined the firm, including Charles Birbeck, who was art director for 50 years, and his half brother William. Many dessert sets can be found today with beautiful hand-painted flowers, birds, and scenes.

From the 1860s through the 1890s, a number of English companies looked to the Far East for inspiration. George Jones was influenced by the Japanese style, and many items, including plates, have storks, bamboo plants, and prunus blossoms in raised gold.

Another decorative technique employed by George Jones was the use of jeweling. Jeweled pieces are highly regarded by collectors today.

George Jones porcelains are comparable to the finest wares ever made and should be considered so by collectors and dealers alike.

LYNTON PORCELAIN COMPANY

The Lynton Porcelain Company is a new china manufactory that began operation in 1982 in Derby, England. The company makes and decorates bone china comparable to some of the finest English pieces produced in the nineteenth century. Lynton plates have superb hand painting with attention to detail, and 24k gold decoration is used. The company broke an age-old tradition by training women to do gilding, traditionally a male-dominated vocation. Using tiny sable brushes, the gilders hand raise designs on pieces of china. The gilders are encouraged to develop their own styles, and each piece is signed by the artist.

MINTON

In 1793 Thomas Minton, with two other partners, opened a pottery in Stoke-on-Trent. For the first few years, blue-printed earthenwares were made that were similar to those made by other companies in the area. In 1798, cream-colored earthenware and bone china were introduced, greatly increasing the sales of the company. During this early period, production was primarily table, tea, and dessert wares. Surviving pattern books show a great variety of printed, enamel-painted, and gilded designs. Subjects were landscapes, chinoiseries, French-inspired floral patterns, lusters, and neoclassical designs.

In the nineteenth century, the artists at Minton produced some spectacular dessert services and show plates. Henry Mitchell specialized in animal subjects, particularly dogs. His works were included in the International Exhibition between 1862 and 1875.

Another famous Minton artist, Antonin Boullemier (1838 – 1900), produced a series of plates with women and children. He was a versatile artist who painted a dessert service with 250 different cherub medallions for the Prince of Wales in 1870.

One of Minton's most important painters during the last quarter of the nineteenth century was Marc-Louis Salon (1835 and 1913). He was born at Montaubon, France, and worked at Sevres between 1851 and 1871. He then brought the pâte-sur-pâte technique to Minton. Pâte-sur-pâte is a very difficult and time-consuming process. The artist traces the outline of a design on an unfired piece of porcelain. He then gradually builds up the desired number of layers of slip, allowing one layer to dry before applying the next. Then the piece is fired. A Minton cabinet plate with pâte-sur-pâte decoration would be a rare treasure today.

WEDGWOOD

The Wedgwood pottery was established in 1759 by Josiah Wedgwood in Stoke-on-Trent. He was born into a family with a long tradition as potters. Wedgwood produced a highly durable cream-colored earthenware that so pleased Queen Charlotte that she appointed him the Royal supplier of dinnerware in 1762.

In 1773, Wedgwood made a set of 1,000 pieces of dinnerware for Catherine II of Russia. This set is referred to as the Frog Service. A different view of England is painted on the central panel of each piece. The rim of each piece is decorated with a pattern of a vine with leaves, which is broken by a crest with a frog. This creature represents the Grenouillère Palace in St. Petersburg. *Grenouillère* is the French word for "frog."

Wedgwood also developed revolutionary ceramic materials such as basalt and jasperware. Josiah Wedgwood is known as "the father of English potters."

THE MANUFACTURE OF WEDGWOOD POTTERY.

THE POTTERS' OVEN.

Emptying the Oven of Fired Ware.

"The Manufacture of Wedgwood Pottery," The Potters' Oven, postcard.

ROYAL WORCESTER

The Worcester pottery was established in 1751 in Worcester, England. It went through many changes in ownership during the next hundred years. William Kerr and R. W. Binns bought the firm in 1852, and the company experienced an artistic recovery. When Kerr left in 1862, the Worcester Royal Porcelain Company, Ltd., was formed. The restyled company made some of the finest porcelain of the Victorian era and competed head to head with the Minton Company in winning top awards at international expositions. Many plate collectors look to this period, which is often referred to as Royal Worcester, for quality show plates to add to their collection. The company was renamed Royal Worcester in 1891.

One of the reasons the Worcester Royal Porcelain Company, Ltd., produced such high-quality porcelain is the number of outstanding artists working for it during that time. The company believed that every porcelain shape was intended, above all, to act as a canvas for fine painting. Today, the cost of employing artists as skilled as these would make the pieces they designed cost prohibitive.

There were numerous Stintons at Royal Worcester through the late nineteenth and early twentieth centuries, with varying degrees of skill. They specialized in painting cattle in misty highland landscapes. Pieces decorated by Stintons bring high prices today.

Harry Davis, one of the best painters at Royal Worcester at the turn of the century, was renowned for his sheep and landscapes. He was more inventive than the Stintons, who repeated the same formula over and over.

Another famous artist with a great following among collectors is Charles Baldwyn. His work is not common and is always of the highest standard. Swans were his favorite bird, and his handling of white was exceptional. An 8½" plate signed by Baldwyn and with swans against a pale blue sky is worth $900.00 – 1,200.00.

Two Worcester artists specializing in landscapes were Raymond Ruston (1886 – 1956), who painted gardens and specialized in pictures of cottages, manor houses, and castles, and Walter Sedgley, who worked for Royal Worcester from 1889 to 1920. Sedgley specialized in flowers and Italian garden scenes. Hilda Everett painted flowers in the 1920s and the 1930s, and George Cole was a fine painter of roses and other flowers around 1912. Frank Roberts (1857 – 1920) painted flowers and fruit and raised gold work. Other fruit painters were Walter Austin (1891 – 1971), who also did flowers, birds, and fish, and Richard Sebright (1868 – 1951). Royal Worcester is still producing fruit-painted plates, which are favorites with American collectors.

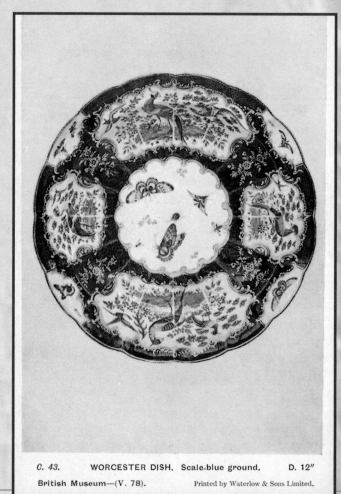

C. 43.   WORCESTER DISH.   Scale-blue ground.   D. 12"

British Museum—(V. 78).   Printed by Waterlow & Sons Limited.

Worcester dish, postcard, British Museum, C. 43.

William Adams & Sons Ltd., Staffordshire Potteries, c. 1879 – 1890. Ironstone, 8³/₄"; Tonquin pattern. $100.00 – 125.00.

William Adams & Sons Ltd., Staffordshire Potteries, c. 1845 – 1864. Earthenware, 10³/₈"; pink and white transfer, home of George Washington, Mt. Vernon. $175.00 – 200.00.

J. G. Alcock, Staffordshire Potteries, c. 1839 – 1846. Plate, 9¹/₂"; Earthenware, 9¹/₂"; blue and white Tyrol pattern. $100.00 – 125.00.

Charles Allerton & Sons, Staffordshire Potteries, c. 1890 – 1900. Child's ABC plate, 6³/₄"; "The Candle Fish." $150.00 – 175.00.

G. L. Ashworth & Bros., Staffordshire Potteries, c. 1884. 9¹/₂"; brown and white transfer, Melrose pattern. $125.00 – 150.00.

Aynsley, c. 1930 – 1950. Scalloped, 8¹/₂"; cobalt and gold. $40.00 – 60.00. (See mark #1.)

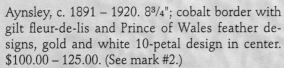

Aynsley, c. 1891 – 1920. 8³/₄"; cobalt border with gilt fleur-de-lis and Prince of Wales feather designs, gold and white 10-petal design in center. $100.00 – 125.00. (See mark #2.)

Aynsley, c. 1891 – 1920. 8¹/₄"; hand-painted castle scene of Loch Lomond, rich cobalt blue border with gilt roses, some scratches on painting. $200.00 – 250.00.

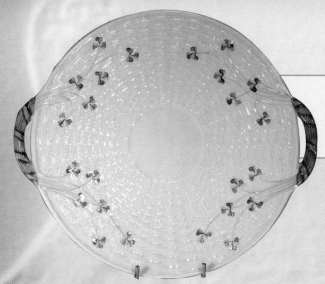

Belleek Pottery Co., David McBirney & Co., Fermanagh, Ireland, 1927 – 1941. Cake plate with two rope-style handles, Shamrock pattern. $175.00 – 200.00.

Belleek Pottery Co., David McBirney & Co., Fermanagh, Ireland, 1980 – 1989. Woven cake plate, round edge, 10$\frac{1}{3}$"; four strands, ivory. $700.00 – 800.00. (See mark #4.)

Belleek Pottery Co., David McBirney & Co., Fermanagh, Ireland, 1921 – 1954. Woven hexagon twig cake plate, 9$\frac{1}{2}$"; four strands, ivory. $900.00 – 1,000.00. (See mark #5.)

Close-up of weaving.

Bishop & Stonier, c. 1891 – 1936. 7"; vivid underglaze blue floral design. $95.00 – 110.00. (See mark #6.)

Another plate, in aqua.

Bodley, c. 1875 – 1892. 9¼"; heavy gold hand-enameled birds and bamboo in Japanese style. $100.00 – 125.00. (See mark #7.)

Close-up of bird.

Bossons, c. 1992. Plasterware plaque, 14"; hand-painted, "Summer Flowers." $75.00 – 100.00.

Bossons, c. 1982. Plasterware plaque, 12"; hand-painted, "Anemones." $75.00 – 100.00.

Bossons, c. 1956 – 1957. Plasterware plaque, 14"; hand-painted, "Westward Ho." $100.00 – 125.00.

Bossons, c. 1956 – 1957. Plasterware plaque, 14"; hand-painted, "Eastgate Chester." $100.00 – 125.00.

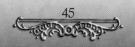

Bossons, c. 1948. Plasterware plaque, 14";
hand-painted, Conway Castle. $75.00 –
100.00. (See mark #8.)

F. D. Bradley, Staffordshire Potteries, c. 1876 – 1896. 9³/₈"; heavy gilt
dragonflies on three handkerchief-style insets, pink ground, Japanese-
style decoration. $250.00 – 300.00.

Sampson Bridgwood & Son, Staffordshire Potteries,
c. 1853 – 1884. Flow Blue, 9¹/₂"; Holy Cross Abbey.
$125.00 – 150.00.

Brownfield & Son, c. 1871 – 1876. 9"; center castle and mountain scene, pink border, gilt decoration on rim. $400.00 – 500.00. (See mark #9.)

Close-up scene.

William Brownfield & Sons, c. 1871 – 1876, made for Tiffany & Co. 9"; hand-painted portrait of Victorian woman. $500.00 – 600.00.

Brown-Westhead, c. 1880 – 1890, made for Davis Collamore & Co., NY. 9¼"; gold enameled birds and flowering tree in Japanese style, blue ground. $100.00 – 125.00. (See mark #10.)

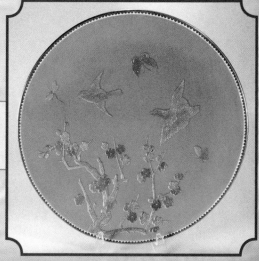

Close-up of lovely yellow rose.

Unmarked, attributed to Brown, Westhead & Moore, c. 1862 – 1904. 9"; well-painted yellow rose, gold and silver leaves. $300.00 – 350.00.

Unmarked, attributed to Brown, Westhead & Moore, c. 1862 – 1904. 9"; well-painted pink rose, gold and silver leaves. $300.00 – 350.00.

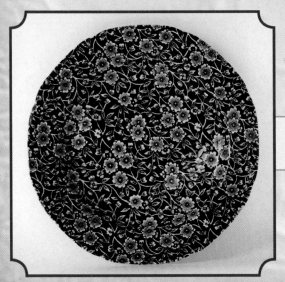

Burgess & Leigh, c. 1930s. Earthenware, 8½"; Calico pattern. $80.00 – 95.00. (See mark #11.)

Cauldon Co., c. 1905 – 1920. Scalloped, 9¹/₂"; exceptionally fine flower painting, heavy gilt and cobalt border. $400.00 – 500.00. (See mark #13.)

Cauldon, c. 1900 – 1920, artist signed "D. Rees." 9¹/₃" with gold gadrooned border; hand-painted flowers in center, pink border with gilt flowers. $200.00 – 250.00.

Cauldon, c. 1905 – 1920, made for Higgins & Seitzer, NY. 10"; gold decoration on white, beaded border. $75.00 – 100.00.

E. Challinor & Co., c. 1853 – 1862. Earthenware, 10"; blue and white transfer, Priory pattern. $150.00 – 175.00. (See mark #14.)

Joseph Clementson, Staffordshire Potteries, c. 1839 – 1864. Ironstone, 8¼"; blue and white transfer of Tillenberg. $150.00 – 200.00.

Coalport, c. 1891 – 1920, made for D. B. Bedell & Co., NY. 9"; center medallion with hand-painted lake scene, ornate gilt decoration with cobalt blue medallions. $400.00 – 500.00. (See mark #15.)

Close-up of lake scene.

Coalport, c. 1891 – 1920, artist signed "J. H. Plant." Plate with gadrooned rim, 9"; hand-painted game birds in center. 150.00 – 200.00.

Coalport, c. 1891 – 1920. Silver-rimmed charger, 11³/₄"; Flower Pot pattern. $100.00 – 150.00.

Coalport, c. 1939 – 1959. Cake plate with two ornate handles, 10" Romany pattern designed by A. Dutton. $100.00 – 125.00. (See mark #16.)

Coalport, c. 1881 – 1890, made for Daniell, London. Reticulated, 9¹/₄"; center medallion of heavy gilt ferns with colorful butterflies, border with three medallions of enameled humming birds on cobalt blue with raised floral and leaf decoration. $600.00 – 700.00. (See mark #17.)

Close-up of border.

Coalport, c. 1891 – 1900, made for Gilman Collamore & Co., New York. 10¼"; exceptional tooled gilding. $400.00 – 500.00.

Coalport, c. 1880 – 1890. 9¼"; well-painted scene of Interlachen, Switzerland, good three-dimensional depth and fine detail. $800.00 – 900.00.

Close-up of scene.

Close-up of figure.

Coalport, c. 1875 –1881; artist signed B. B. 9$^{1}/_{3}$"; hand-painted figure of lady in a beautiful gown holding a basket of flowers in a seaside setting, elaborate border with raised gilt beads and flowers and reticulated entwined flowers. $1,000.00 – 1,200.00. (See mark #18.)

Coalport, c. 1881 – 1890. Scalloped and ribbed, 9$^{3}/_{8}$"; hand-painted cherry blossoms and butterflies, gilt on rim. $125.00 – 150.00.

Coalport, c. 1960 – present. Scalloped, 8"; India Tree Blue pattern. $75.00 – 90.00. (See mark #19.)

Coalport, c. 1875 – 1881. 9", with reticulated border; underglaze blue printed pattern. $150.00 – 175.00.

Coalport, c. 1875 – 1881. 10"; underglaze blue printed pattern. $100.00 – 125.00.

Coalport, c. 1875 – 1881. 8¼", with pearl-jeweled rim; underglaze blue printed pattern. $100.00 – 125.00.

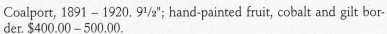

Coalport, 1891 – 1920. 9½"; hand-painted fruit, cobalt and gilt border. $400.00 – 500.00.

Coalport, 1891 – 1920. Two-handled platter, 11¹⁄₄"; hand-painted fruit. $500.00 – 600.00.

Close-up of fruit.

Coalport, c. 1820 – 1825. Feltspar, 9¹⁄₄"; hand-painted fruit and flowers, tan border with white relief flowers. $700.00 – 800.00. (See mark #20.)

Close-up of fruit and flowers.

Copeland Spode, c. 1891 – 1920, artist signed "I. Arrowsmith," made for Tiffany & Co., New York. Plate, 8³/₄"; hand-painted flowers in center, three floral medallions framed in gold, black matte ground. $75.00 – 100.00. (See mark #22.)

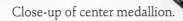

Close-up of center medallion.

Copeland Spode, c. 1878, artist signed "H. Lea." Presentation plate, 9¹/₃"; array of hand-painted flowers. $400.00 – 450.00. (See mark #23.)

Copeland Spode, c. 1851 – 1885, artist signed "CLA." 9½"; amateur-decorated plate with stippling technique, portrait of young girl with veil, necklace girl wears is enameled. $200.00 – 250.00. (See mark #24.)

Copeland Spode, c. 1851 – 1885, artist signed "CLA." 9½"; amateur-decorated plate with stippling technique, portrait of young girl with ruffled bonnet. $200.00 – 250.00.

Copeland Spode, c. 1891, artist signed "Samuel Alcock." 9"; hand-painted portrait of lady by famous Copeland portrait artist Samuel Alcock, exquisite border with turquoise, coral, and gold jeweling and gold roses. $600.00 – 700.00.

Close-up of portrait.

Close-up of jeweled border.

Copeland Spode, c. 1891 – 1920. 8³/₄"; jeweled border, coat-of-arms center. $200.00 – 250.00.

Copeland Spode, c. 1891 – 1920. Service plate, 10½"; rich cobalt blue ground with heavy beaded gilt and jeweling. $350.00 – 400.00.

Close-up of jeweling.

Copeland Spode, c. 1890s, made for A. B. Daniell & Son, London, artist signed "Samuel Alcock." 9⅛"; hand-painted portrait of "Gainsborough head," pearl and turquoise jeweling and gold beading on border. $600.00 – 700.00.

Close-up of portrait.

Copeland Spode, c. 1890s, made for A. B. Daniell & Son, London, artist signed "Samuel Alcock." 9$\frac{1}{8}$"; hand-painted portrait of "Gainsborough head," pearl and turquoise jeweling and gold beading on border. $600.00 – 700.00.

Copeland Spode, c. 1890s, made for A. B. Daniell & Son, London, artist signed "Samuel Alcock." 9$\frac{1}{8}$"; hand-painted portrait of "Gainsborough head," pearl and turquoise jeweling and gold beading on border. $600.00 – 700.00.

Copeland Spode, c. 1877. Richelieu shape, 9"; hand-painted flowers, border with gilt and pearl jeweling. $400.00 – 500.00.

Copeland Spode, c. 1890s. Unusual shape, 9"; rich cobalt blue with raised gold flowers and leaves in center, border loaded with gold beads and pearl jeweling. $300.00 – 400.00.

Copeland Spode, c. 1862 – 1891, artist signed "C. F. Hürten." 8³/₄"; realistic array of flowers and buds in center by one of the best flower artists of all time. $1,500.00 – 1,800.00.

Copeland Spode, c. 1851 – 1885. 9¹/₈"; hand-painted pink and blue morning glories with aqua border and decorated gold rim. $150.00 – 200.00.

Copeland Spode, c. 1883. Dessert plate, 7"; underglaze blue flowers, gold border with cobalt fruit and flower decoration. $125.00 – 150.00. (See mark #25.)

Copeland Spode, c. 1875 – 1890. 8¹/₄"; stylized cobalt flowers on gilt. $200.00 – 250.00. (See mark #26.)

Copeland Spode, c. 1850 – 1867. Earthenware, 10"; blue and white transfer. $100.00 – 125.00.

Copeland Spode, c. 1891 – 1900. Scalloped, 8¼"; cobalt ground, stylized white flowers, gilt trim. $150.00 – 175.00.

Copeland Spode, c. 1890s, artist signed "Samuel Alcock." 9¼"; figure of woman, heavily jeweled border. $800.00 – 1,000.00.

Close-up of border.

Copeland Spode, c. 1883. 8¼"; heavy jeweling on dark green. $400.00 – 500.00.

Copeland Spode, c. 1891, artist signed "H. C. Lea." 9¾"; hand-painted fish in center, aqua border with gold crosses. $300.00 – 400.00.

Copeland Spode, c. 1891, made for Ovington Bros., New York. 9"; hand-painted flowers in center, swirled gilt ferns, jewels, and medallions of hand-painted flowers. $500.00 – 600.00. (See mark #27.)

Copeland Spode, c. 1872 – 1879, artist signed "Lucien Besche." Charger, 12", hand-painted portrait of Dutch oil-on-canvas painter Adrian Van Ostade. $500.00 – 600.00.

Close-up of signature.

Copeland Spode, c. 1879, artist signed "C. F. H." (Hurten). 9"; incredible hand-painted luscious fully ripened peony. $2,000.00 – 2,500.00.

Close-up of flower.

Copeland Spode, c. 1879. 9"; hand-painted cherries and goose-berries attributed to Charles F. Hurten, pink border with tooled raised paste gilding. $1,200.00 – 1,500.00.

Close-up of fruit.

Davenport, Staffordshire Potteries, c. 1820 – 1860. Ironstone, 9"; black transfer, scene of Cyprus. $200.00 – 250.00.

Davenport, c. 1820 – 1860. 7¼"; Indian Scroll pattern. $175.00 – 200.00.

Royal Crown Derby, c. 1878 – 1890, artist initialed "E. F." 9¼"; hand-painted portrait of a dog. $800.00 – 900.00.

Royal Crown Derby, c. 1878 – 1890, artist initialed "E. F." 9¼"; hand-painted portrait of a dog. $800.00 – 900.00.

Close-up of dog.

Royal Crown Derby, c. 1878 – 1890. 9⅛"; cobalt border with six floral medallions outlined with gold beads, array of hand-painted flowers in center. $500.00 – 600.00. (See mark #28.)

Royal Crown Derby, c. 1885. 8²/₃"; heavy gold basket and casket with cascading enameled pink flowers with jewel centers, heavy gold border. $400.00 – 500.00.

Crown Ducal (A. G. Richardson), c. 1925 – 1930. Earthenware, 8"; Blue Chintz pattern. $125.00 – 150.00.

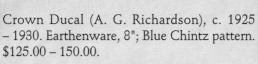

Doulton, Burslem, c. 1887. Scalloped, 8³/₄"; cobalt leaves, gilt sponge wear effect. $75.00 – 100.00. (See mark #29.)

Royal Doulton, c. 1937, made for Ovington Brothers. Service plate, 10¹/₂"; elaborate gilt decoration. $75.00 – 100.00. (See mark #30.)

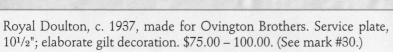

Doulton, Burslem, c. 1891 – 1902. Reticulated, 9"; six swirled medallions with daisies. $150.00 – 175.00.

Doulton, Burslem, c. 1891 – 1902. Reticulated, 9"; six swirled medallions with yellow and blue flowers. $150.00 – 175.00.

Doulton, Burslem, c. 1887. Scalloped, 8³⁄₄"; transfer cobalt blue flowers, gilt. $75.00 – 100.00.

Doulton, Burslem, c. 1887. Intricately scalloped, 8³⁄₄"; hand-painted pastel leaves outlined in gold. $125.00 – 150.00.

Doulton, Burslem, c. 1887. Intricately scalloped, 8³/₄"; hand-painted pastel leaves outlined in gold. $125.00 – 150.00.

Doulton, Burslem, c. 1890s. 8¹/₂"; transfer pink and blue flowers. $50.00 – 60.00.

Doulton, Burslem, c. 1890s. 8¹/₂"; hand-painted pink and blue mums. $75.00 – 100.00.

Royal Doulton, c. 1910 – 1915, artist signed "C. Hart," made for Bailey, Banks & Biddle, Philadelphia, PA. 8³/₄"; portrait of black grouse and his mate, ¹/₂" gold border. $300.00 – 350.00. (See mark #31.)

Royal Doulton, c. 1902 – 1920, imported by George Bowman Co., Cleveland. Earthenware, 10¼"; blue and white transfer of Mt. Vernon. $100.00 – 150.00.

Royal Doulton, c. 1902 – 1920. Service plate, 10¼"; cobalt border, lavish gilt. $300.00 – 350.00.

Royal Doulton, c. 1907. Service plate, 10¼"; cobalt border with gilt decoration. $300.00 – 350.00.

Royal Doulton, c. 1911. Service plate, 10½"; raised gilt decoration on border, gold-etched rim. $350.00 – 400.00.

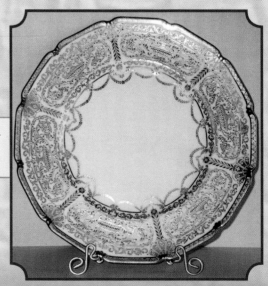

Doulton Burslem, c. 1891 – 1902. Scalloped, 9"; experimental technique of photograph of Doulton porcelain artist. $300.00 – 350.00.

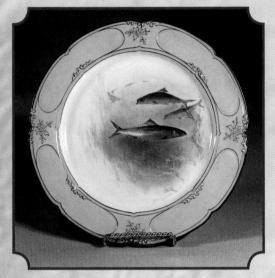

Royal Doulton, c. 1920 – 1930. 9¼"; hand-painted fish. $200.00 – 250.00.

Doulton Burslem, c. 1879, impressed Pinder Bourne mark. Majolica charger, 19¼"; arrangement of applied irises and small daisies. $900.00 – 1,000.00.

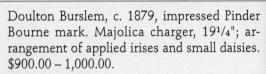

Close-up of flowers.

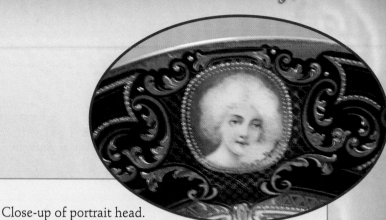

Close-up of portrait head.

Royal Doulton, c. 1900 – 1904, artist signed "Antonin Boullemier," made for Gillman & Collamore, NY. Service plate, 10¼"; cobalt and raised gold border, portrait-head medallion of a woman on border. $500.00 – 600.00.

Elin, Knight & Bridgwood, Staffordshire Potteries, c. 1827 – 1840. Earthenware, 10¼"; blue and white transfer, Chinese Fountains. $150.00 – 200.00.

W. H. Grindley & Co., c. 1891 – 1914. Flow Blue, 10"; cobalt blue center and border, gilt trim. $90.00 – 110.00.

John Hall & Sons, c. 1822 – 1932. Earthenware, 9³/₄"; dark blue and white transfer, Oriental scene. $200.00 – 250.00.

Hammersley, c. 1887 – 1912, made for Ovington Bros., New York. 9¹/₈"; gilt scrolling or monogram in center, garland of flowers, heavy raised gold floral border. $75.00 – 100.00. (See mark #45.)

Hammersley, c. 1912 – 1939, artist signed "F. A. Marple." 8¹/₂"; beautifully painted birds in scenic setting in center, peach, pale yellow and cream border with gold leaves with pearl enameled centers. $250.00 – 300.00. (See mark #46.)

Hammersley, c. 1912 – 1939, artist signed "F. A. Marple." 8½"; beautifully painted bird in scenic setting in center, peach, pale yellow and cream border with gold leaves with pearl enameled centers. $250.00 – 300.00.

Close-up of bird.

Hammersley, c. 1912 – 1939, artist signed "F. A. Marple." 8½"; beautifully painted birds in scenic setting in center; peach, pale yellow, and cream border with gold leaves with pearl enameled centers. $250.00 – 300.00.

Hammersley, c. 1912 – 1939, artist signed "F. A. Marple." 8½"; beautifully painted bird in scenic setting in center; peach, pale yellow and cream border with gold leaves with pearl enameled centers. $250.00 – 300.00.

Johnson Bros., Staffordshire Potteries, c. 1900. Flow Blue, 9½";
Normandy pattern. $125.00 – 150.00.

Johnson Bros., Staffordshire Potteries, c. 1913+.
Flow Blue, 9½"; Warwich pattern. $100.00
– 125.00. (See mark #52.)

Johnson Bros., c. 1900 – 1910. Flow Blue, 8"; Claremont.
$100.00 – 125.00.

George Jones, c. 1880. 7¾"; excellent hand-painted
flowers, gilt and cobalt border. $200.00 – 250.00.

George Jones, c. 1880. 7³/4"; excellent hand-painted flowers, gilt and cobalt border. $200.00 – 250.00.

George Jones, c. 1880. 7³/4"; excellent hand-painted flowers, gilt and cobalt border. $200.00 – 250.00.

George Jones, c. 1880. 7³/4"; excellent hand-painted flowers, gilt and cobalt border. $200.00 – 250.00.

George Jones, c. 1924 – 1951. Scalloped game plate, 8⁵/8"; hand-painted peacocks center, lovely border of roses on gilt. $300.00 – 400.00.

George Jones, c. 1854 – 1860. Earthenware, 9¼"; lavender transfer, "Costumers Espanoles." $200.00 – 250.00.

Lynton Porcelain Co., c. 1982 – present. 9"; hand-painted center scene, black border with raised gold decoration. $400.00 – 500.00. (See mark #88.)

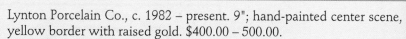

Lynton Porcelain Co., c. 1982 – present. 9"; hand-painted center scene, yellow border with raised gold. $400.00 – 500.00.

Mayer & Sherratt, c. 1921 – 1925. Scalloped, 8"; underglaze blue floral pattern. $80.00 – 95.00.

Mellor, Venables & Co., Staffordshire Potteries, c. 1834 – 1851. Ironstone, 8½"; blue and white transfer, Medici. $250.00 – 300.00.

Minton, c. 1873 – 1890. 9½", gadrooned border; hand-painted castle scene. $250.00 – 300.00. (See mark #94.)

Minton, c. 1894, artist signed "Antonin Boullemier," made for T. Goode & Co., London. Plate with reticulated border, 9¼"; center painting of little girl feeding birds. $1,500.00 – 1,700.00. (See mark #95.)

Close-up.

Minton, c. 1873 – 1890. 9½"; exceptional border with intricate gold and silver work, gilt reserves framed by red enamel dots, hand-painted white flowers in center with turquoise ground. $700.00 – 800.00.

Close-up of border.

Close-up.

Minton, c. 1890 – 1895, made for T. Goode & Co., London. 9½"; pink ground with raised white enameled birds perched on a flowering branch, attributed to famous artist Desiré Leroy, gilt and pierced border. $1,200.00 – 1,400.00.

Minton, c. 1879, artist signed "A. Boullemier." Plate, 9½"; well-painted figure of lovely young woman picking flowers, pierced gilded and beaded border. $1,400.00 – 1,600.00.

Close-up of figure.

Close-up.

Minton, c. 1872, artist signed "Henry Mitchell." 9⅓"; fine painting of an adorable dog who knows he has done something naughty, raised gilt border with turquoise rim. $1,000.00 – 1,200.00.

Minton, c. 1880. 9¹/₈"; charming hand-painted scene of dog, attributed to Henry Mitchell, white enameled leaves on turquoise border. $900.00 – 1,000.00.

Close-up.

Minton, c. 1902 – 1911, made special for Tiffany & Co., artist signed "Albert H. Wright" and rare gilder's signature, "S. J. Russell." Plate, 9"; entitled "Oyster Catcher," rare hand-painted bird plate with exceptional raised gilding on border. $3,000.00 – 4,000.00. (See mark #96.)

Close-up of birds.

Close-up of gilder's signature.

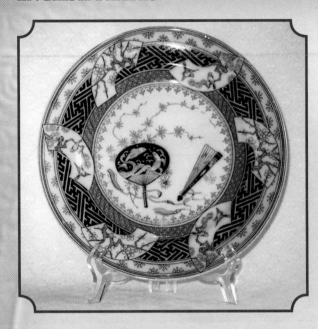

Minton, c. 1876. 10³/₈"; Bombay pattern. $150.00 – 200.00.

Minton, c. 1917, made for Tiffany & Co., NY. Service plate, 10¼"; cobalt border with gilt decoration and monogram, red diamonds with gilt. $350.00 – 400.00.

Minton, c. 1942, made for Tiffany & Co., NY. Service plate, 10¼"; cobalt border with gilt decoration, gold etched rim. $300.00 – 325.00.

Minton, c. 1873 – 1875, made special for Caldwell & Co., Philadelphia, PA, attributed to Henry Mitchell. 9¼", wonderful reticulated beaded border; hand-painted water buffalo in manner of Edwin Landseer, famous painter of animals (1802 – 1873), turquoise ground. $700.00 – 800.00.

Close-up.

Minton, c. 1873 – 1890, made for T. Goode & Co., London. 9¼"; hand-painted portrait of a Cupid holding on to a bouquet of large pink and yellow roses. $500.00 – 550.00. (See mark #97.)

Close-up of Cupid.

Minton, c. 1863 – 1872, made for John Mortlock Co., London. 9¼"; hand-painted orchids on pale green ground, reticulated border with white daisies. $350.00 – 400.00.

Minton, c. 1870 – 1880s, artist signed "W. Mussill." 9½"; realistic painting of lobster. $500.00 – 600.00.

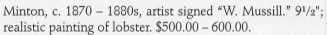

Close-up.

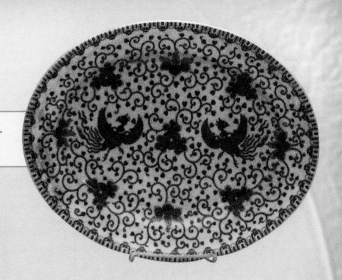

Myott & Son, c. 1930s. 12½" x 10"; Satsuma pattern. $65.00 – 80.00.

New Wharf Pottery Co., Staffordshire Potteries, c. 1890 – 1894. Flow Blue, 10"; Conway pattern. $100.00 – 125.00. (See mark #98.)

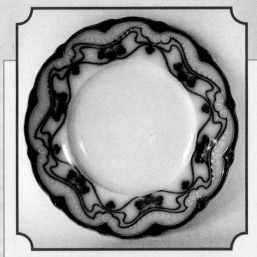

New Wharf Pottery Co., Staffordshire Potteries, c. 1890 – 1894. Flow Blue, 9"; Paris pattern. $80.00 – 95.00.

William Ridgway & Co., Staffordshire Potteries, c. 1834 – 1854. 9¾"; black and white transfer Grecian pattern. $150.00 – 200.00.

John Rogers & Sons, Staffordshire Potteries, c. 1814 – 1836. Earthenware, 9⅝"; dark blue historical transfer. $300.00 – 350.00.

Shelley, c. 1925 – 1940. Hors d'oeuvres plate with handle in middle, 11"; Dainty Blue pattern. $200.00 – 250.00. (See mark #141.)

Thomas Till, c. 1870 – 1890. 9¼"; blue transfer scene. $100.00 – 125.00.

John Wedge Wood, c. 1848 registration mark. Ironstone, 9⅛"; blue and white transfer, some staining. $100.00 – 150.00.

Wedgwood, c. 1850. Earthenware, 9¹/₂"; blue
transfer scene. $200.00 – 250.00.

Wedgwood, c. 1891 – 1900. Earthenware, 9¹/₄";
purple and white transfer, Ferrara. $150.00 – 200.00.

Wedgwood, c. 1906 – 1920. Earthenware, 9¹/₄"; blue and white transfer, Oriental scene. $100.00 – 150.00.

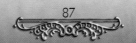

Wedgwood, c. 1878 – 1891. 9¹⁄₄"; painting of girl with blue bonnet holding a toy soldier, unique gilt decoration. $400.00 – 450.00. (See mark #157.)

Close-up.

Whittaker & Co., Staffordshire Potteries, c. 1886. Earthenware, 8"; brown and white transfer Oriental flowers and screen motif. $60.00 – 75.00.

Whittingham, Ford & Co., Staffordshire Potteries, c. 1868 – 1873. Earthenware with gadrooned border, 9"; blue and white transfer scene. $100.00 – 150.00.

James F. Wileman, c. 1869 – 1892. 7"; underglaze blue design. $80.00 – 95.00.

A. J. Wilkinson Ltd, Staffordshire Potteries, c. 1907. Earthenware, 8"; red and white transfer of scene. $100.00 – 125.00.

Enoch Wood & Sons, c. 1818 – 1846. Earthenware, 9¼"; historical blue and white transfer, East view of La Grange, seat of Marquis de Lafayette. $400.00 – 500.00.

Enoch Wood & Sons, c. 1818 – 1846. Earthenware, 8$\frac{1}{2}$"; dark blue and white transfer, American historical scene. $350.00 – 400.00.

Set of 12 plates. Royal Worcester, c. 1937, artist signed "H. Powell." 4$\frac{1}{2}$" each; hand-painted birds on tree branches. $1,200.00 – 1,400.00.

Royal Worcester, c. 1932, artist signed. 9$\frac{1}{4}$"; hand-painted fish. $400.00 – 450.00.

Close-up of center.

Royal Worcester, c. 1938, artist signed "Price," made for Mappin & Webb. Service plate, 10¼"; hand-painted fruit in center, cobalt border with lavish gilt decoration. $400.00 – 450.00. (See mark #161.)

Royal Worcester, c. 1908, made for Greenleaf & Crosby Company. 9⅝"; blue and white transfer of Old City Gate in St. Augustine, Florida. $100.00 – 150.00. (See mark #162.)

Royal Worcester, c. 1850s. Charger, 14½"; hand-painted bird and flowering tree. $400.00 – 500.00.

Royal Worcester, c. 1900. 9½"; raised gold wheat decoration, pearl-jeweled rim. $200.00 – 250.00.

Royal Worcester, c. 1883. 8¾"; underglaze blue roses and scroll decoration. $125.00 – 150.00.

Royal Worcester, c. 1883. 10½"; underglaze hand-painted blue bird and branch. $125.00 – 150.00.

Royal Worcester, c. 1882. 9"; hand-painted flowers on pink ground. $300.00 – 350.00. (See mark #163.)

Royal Worcester, c. 1929, artist signed "E. Phillips." $8^2/_3$"; jeweled border with gilt flowers, array of hand-painted flowers in center. $300.00 – 350.00. (See mark #164.)

Close-up.

Royal Worcester, c. 1880. 9"; botanical plate, hand-painted flowering branch, blue and gilt border. $250.00 – 300.00.

Royal Worcester, c. 1881. 9"; hand-painted flowers, pink and gilt border. $300.00 – 375.00.

Close-up.

Royal Worcester, c. 1936. Octagonal plate, 10½"; hand-painted portrait of a St. Bernard dog with the motto "Perge sed caute," which means "Proceed but with caution." Made exclusively for exclusive all-male St. Bernard's School in NYC, founded in 1904. $400.00 – 500.00.

Royal Worcester, c. 1884, made special for Theodore B. Starr, New York. 9"; hand-painted bird in natural setting; pink border with white and gold jewels. $200.00 – 250.00.

George Grainger & Co., Worcester, c. 1889 – 1902. Deeply scalloped, 6⅞"; hand-painted flowers, heavy gilt border. $150.00 – 175.00.

Unidentified maker, Staffordshire Potteries, c. 1830 – 1850. Scalloped earthenware, 10³/₈"; rare purple transfer of Venetian scene, beautiful urn and flower border. $400.00 – 500.00.

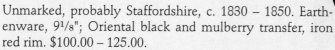

Unmarked, probably Staffordshire, c. 1830 – 1850. Earthenware, 9¹/₈"; Oriental black and mulberry transfer, iron red rim. $100.00 – 125.00.

Unmarked, probably Staffordshire, c. 1880s. Scalloped earthenware, 9¹/₄"; Flow Blue floral. $75.00 – 100.00.

Unidentified, Staffordshire Potteries, c. 1909. Earthenware, 9"; dark blue and white transfer, Washington D. C. buildings. $75.00 – 100.00.

Marked "England," Staffordshire Potteries, c. 1830 – 1850s. Earthenware, 9¼"; dark blue and white transfer, "Views of Minneapolis." $150.00 – 200.00.

Unidentified mark, Staffordshire Potteries, c. 1840s. Earthenware, 9¼"; early mulberry transferware, Fruit Basket pattern. $150.00 – 200.00.

Unidentified mark, Staffordshire Potteries, c. 1850s. Earthenware, 7⅝"; red transferware scene. $125.00 – 175.00.

Unidentified mark, Staffordshire Potteries, c. 1890 – 1910. Flow Blue, 9¼"; scenes of Atlantic City. $100.00 – 125.00.

Unidentified maker, Staffordshire Potteries, distributed by George H. Bowman Co., NY and Cleveland, c. 1900. Earthenware, 10"; blue and white transfer, Molly Pitcher at Battle of Monmouth, June 28, 1776. $100.00 – 125.00.

English, unknown maker, c. 1890s. 9$\frac{1}{3}$"; hand-painted flowers, dark red border with gilt flowers and butterflies. $200.00 – 250.00.

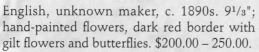

English, unknown maker, c. 1890s. 9"; hand-painted strawberries and flowers, jeweled red and green border. $200.00 – 250.00.

Close-up.

Unidentified company, marked "made in England." Cake plate with two handles, 10½"; floral chintz pattern. $80.00 – 95.00.

Unidentified maker, unreadable impressed mark, c. 1890 – 1900. 8"; underglaze blue birds and branches in aesthetic style. $75.00 – 100.00.

English, unmarked, c. 1850 – 1870. 7⅝"; floral cartouches on cobalt and gilt ground. $200.00 – 250.00.

English, unmarked, c. 1900. Plate, 9¼" hand painting of Scottish loch, pink border. $150.00 – 175.00.

English, unmarked, c. 1880 – 1900. 9¼"; hand-painted irises in center, gilt cartouches on pink border. $250.00 – 300.00.

English, unmarked, c. 1890. 9"; hand-painted castle scene in style of Coalport artist J. H. Plant's castle views, gold-beaded lariat-type decoration on pink border. $250.00 – 300.00.

Close-up of castle scene.

English, unmarked, c. 1890s. 9¹/₄"; hand-painted daisies, butterfly. $150.00 – 200.00.

English, unmarked, c. 1890s. 9¹/₄"; hand-painted violets, butterflies. $150.00 – 200.00.

KELLER & GUERIN

Keller & Guerin bought an old faience factory in Luneville, France, in 1778. The company made faience, and at the end of the nineteenth century also made an English-style earthenware. The company made many oyster plates that are eagerly collected today.

LIMOGES PORCELAIN PLATES — CANVASES FOR FINE PAINTING

Limoges porcelain has had a place in the TIAS (The Internet Antique Shop) "Hot List" of Antiques and Collectibles since the list was first published in 2002. The search word *Limoges* is currently number three on the Antique Arts websight, which specializes in high-end antiques.

In addition to the lovely dinnerware services and decorative accessories made in Limoges, the magnificent hand-painted plates and chargers are eagerly sought by collectors. These items beautifully showcase the extraordinary talents of the French and American professional artists, as well as the talented American home painters of the late nineteenth century.

LIMOGES, THE CENTER OF HARD-PASTE PORCELAIN PRODUCTION

In *Godden's Guide to European Porcelains*, Geoffrey Godden says, "Limoges is to France as Stoke-on-Trent is to England — the center of the ceramic industry." Limoges is about 200 miles southwest of Paris and owes its prominence in the field of hard-paste porcelain production in France to the abundance of natural resources. The soil in the area is rich in deposits of kaolin and feldspar, the essential ingredients for hard-paste porcelain. The region also has forests to supply necessary fuel for the kilns, and rivers to provide easy transportation for the finished goods.

Some porcelain was made at Limoges from the 1780s by Massie, Fourniere, and Giellet, who worked under the royal protection of the Comte D'Artois. However, most of the kaolin was supplied to the Sevres Company and Paris-based porcelain manufacturers in the late eighteenth and early nineteenth centuries. The porcelain industry in the Limoges area employed about 200 workers around 1807. By 1830, the number had increased to over 1,800 employees. The period of the mid-to-late 1800s was the golden age of the Limoges porcelain industry.

Production became industrialized, and new methods of manufacturing and decoration were introduced. To meet the growing demand of a large export market, new mass production techniques were introduced. Approximately 75% of the porcelain was exported, the largest percentage to the United States. In 1900, 18,000 barrels of decorated and blank porcelain were shipped from the Limoges factories to the United States. The number of the companies increased from 32 in the late 1800s to 48 in the 1920s, and entire families were employed, as many jobs could be accomplished by women and children.

Hand-painted plates, chargers, and plaques made by Limoges companies were in demand by the American consumer. These porcelain items were not cheap for the times, but they were still in demand. Victoriana dictated the tastes of the period, and Americans had elaborate lifestyles. The homes were furnished and decorated quite lavishly when compared to today's standards.

With the tremendous amount of porcelain produced, the market couldn't absorb all the wares. After World War I and the economic depressions of the 1920s and 1930s, many older companies were forced out of business. There was some revitalization after World War II, and today Limoges is still the center of hard-paste porcelain production in France.

At the time of Limoges's golden age of porcelain, there were as many as 48 companies. Most of them included decorative plates and chargers in their inventories. Some companies, such as the famous Haviland firms, concentrated their efforts primarily on dinnerware. A brief history of those companies who frequently manufactured and/or decorated chargers and wall plaques is listed below. The first and second editions of Mary Frank Gaston's *The Collector's Encyclopedia of Limoges Porcelain* were most helpful in providing this information.

The Companies

A number of companies located in Limoges made and decorated fine cabinet plates as well as dinnerware. A few are listed below.

Blakeman & Henderson (B & H)

Blakeman & Henderson (B & H) imported porcelain to the United States during the 1890s and the early 1900s. Its decoration was always of the highest quality. Its portrait chargers were dramatic and often embellished with heavy gold borders.

Borgfeldt, George

The George Borgfeldt studio was located in Paris; however, it decorated porcelain made by several companies in Limoges, especially the Coiffe Company. Several famous French artists did work for Borgfeldt, including Dubois, Luc, and Armond. Popular subjects were fruit, courting scenes, and cavaliers.

Demartine & Cie

Demartine & Cie was in operation from 1891 to the early 1900s. An outstanding example of its work is a portrait plate of Mrs. Sheridan after Gainsborough, painted by J. Soustre, one of the best French figure painters of the time.

Flambeau China

Flambeau China operated from the 1890s until 1910, first as a decorator and then as a producer of porcelain. Its specialty was fish and game sets. Duca and Gilbert were two artists who painted for the company.

The William Guerin Company

The William Guerin Company went through many management changes and was in operation from the 1870s through 1932. The company produced game and fish sets and floral and figural chargers. One of the best examples of its work is a large charger showing a family having tea.

The Haviland Family

The Haviland family had several porcelain companies and decorating studios in France and the United States. Many wonderful cabinet and oyster plates were produced. Of special interest is a series of Sevres-style plates of French court ladies. They also decorated plates with fruits and flowers.

The Lazeyras, Rosenfeld, Lehman (LRL)

The Lazeyras, Rosenfeld, Lehman (LRL) firm operated in around the 1920s. It specialized in game and fish sets. It also painted flowers, fruit, figures, and hand-painted courting scenes. Artists used by the company in the mid-1930s were Muville and J. Soustre.

The Pouyat Company

The Pouyat Company has a long history in the porcelain business, beginning in 1760. It produced a large amount of whiteware that was sold to the United States for decoration, as well as dinnerware and some beautiful cabinetware. It decorated chargers with dramatic flowers, fruit, and courting scenes.

Tressemann & Vogt (T & V)

Tressemann & Vogt (T & V) formed in the 1880s. It sold whiteware blanks to the United States for china painting by American decorating studios and home painters. It decorated plates with figures in the Art Nouveau style, as well as fish and game sets, flowers, landscapes, and courting scenes.

LIMOGES CHARGERS ARE UNIQUE WORKS OF ART

There are three characteristics found in Limoges plaques and chargers that give them a very rich appearance and set them apart from all others. First is the purity and translucency of the porcelain itself. Many blanks are exquisitely molded with floral decorations, beading, and scalloped edges to show off the beauty of the porcelain body.

Second is the magnificent gold embellishment used by the Limoges companies. The gold, referred to as coin gold, was lavishly applied to plaques and chargers and other decorative objects during the height of the golden age of porcelain in Limoges, France. The gold has a rich patina and was used on the borders to frame the lovely painting, thus creating a work of art to match any oil or watercolor painting on canvas.

Third, the deep and vibrantly colored artwork gives the objects a very rich appearance and make a striking contrast with the gold border. Gaston says, "It is this image that comes to mind when one says Limoges."

The subjects used on Limoges chargers by both the factory artists and home painters were varied, and decorating styles were influenced by the artistic movements at the time. The height of the Art Nouveau period coincided with the height of the golden age of Limoges porcelain — the late 1880s through 1905. The name *Art Nouveau* is French for "new art" and is derived from the 1895 opening of a design shop in Paris. The movement is characterized by flowing, sensuous lines; the feminine form; swirling leaf and floral motifs; and fruits, especially grapes and insects.

Floral decoration is the most frequently found subject on Limoges plates and chargers, and professional paintings of roses are popular with collectors today. Brilliant red poppies, lush orchids, and multicolored dahlias were also favorite flowers used by the porcelain artists. Fruit themes were also popular, and colorful berries; cherries; grapes; red, green, or golden apples; and plump peaches decorate chargers.

Elaborate oyster, fish, and game services were used at the dinner table in Victorian America. Many of the artists who painted these sets, such as Dubois, Henriot, and Rene, also decorated beautiful chargers.

Figural themes, both portrait and allegorical, as well as scenic decor, are less common subjects on Limoges porcelain and are eagerly collected. Portraitware was popular during the mid-nineteenth century. Male subjects included important historical figures, such as Napoleon and Louis XVI. Most portraits featured beautiful women, however, ranging from the French Empress Josephine to unknown Victorian women. Some of the most highly prized Limoges decorated chargers are those having Art Nouveau–style ladies with elaborate gowns and with grape clusters in their flowing hair. Sometimes a sleek tiger or greyhound dog completed the portrait.

There is probably no other group of porcelains having such a tremendous range of subject matter and painted by such a variety of professional and amateur artists as those made by the Limoges companies. Plates and chargers are available to fit all budgets, and each one is truly a work of art.

INFORMATION FOR THE COLLECTOR

When collecting Limoges porcelain, certain factors should be considered, such as the age of the piece, the beauty and skill of the workmanship, and the decorating style.

Limoges porcelains are still in production, and as a general rule, the quality of the craftsmanship and decoration on older pieces is superior to new examples. Less gold is used on newer pieces, and few are completely hand painted. Newer marks are usually over the glaze.

As a general guideline, marks using "Limoges" can be dated to 1860 or later. Marks including "France"

generally date the piece 1891 onwards, and the use of "Made in France" means the piece was made after 1914.

The first, second, and third editions of *The Collector's Encyclopedia of Limoges Porcelain* by Mary Frank Gaston are essential tools for any collector or dealer of Limoges porcelains. Her section on marks is particularly helpful. Gaston explains that factory marks are usually green and stamped under the glaze. These are called whiteware marks. There can also be marks to show factory or studio decoration, importers, exporters, and artists. These marks (often red) are usually over the glaze. American decorating studios, such as the Pickard Company, placed their marks with their names on the pieces they decorated. Professional artists' signatures are usually found on the fronts of the pieces. Sometimes they are hidden, and you must look closely to find them. Some artists used special marks on the backs of the pieces. Many times there will be a name and date on the back of a piece. This type of signature is common on whitewares decorated by nonprofessional artists.

Limoges chargers that carry both decorators' marks and artists' signatures are usually the most desirable pieces. The exquisite items decorated at the Pickard studio would be included in this group. Next in demand are those pieces hand painted and with decorators' marks but without artists' signatures. Finally, the last and largest group are the numerous chargers and plates that are home decorated. These items are often quite beautiful and unique and should be judged on their individual merits. Decorative plates and chargers made by the Limoges companies are very recognizable. With a little knowledge and hands-on experience, anyone can become a serious Limoges collector.

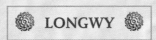

LONGWY

Longwy Pottery began operation in 1798 and is located in Lorraine, France. In 1875, Emaux de Longwy introduced wares that were decorated with Orientally inspired designs, cloisonné enamels in particular. His designs were outlined in black and then filled in with bril-

liantly colored glazes, especially the turquoise color for which the pieces are most famous. Examples are marked "LONGWY," either printed under the glaze or impressed. Many Longwy items have a uniform crazing, which doesn't take away from the value.

PARIS PORCELAIN

Paris porcelains are made from hard paste and were made or decorated in the city of Paris or environs from the 1770s until the late nineteenth century. The name Old Paris (*vieux Paris*) is a term coined by antique dealers in the United States in the late nineteenth century. It reflects the location of many of the Paris porcelain factories in the northeast, or old part, of the city, which was a well-known artisans' quarter.

Right from the beginning, the Parisian manufacturers were highly regarded by members of royalty. Emperor Napoleon I subsidized several companies and awarded them important commissions. His favorites were Jean Nast (1754 – 1817) and Pierre-Louis Dagoty (1771 – 1840).

Some exquisite cabinet plates were produced in Paris, partly due to the emergence of trade fairs in England and Europe. Paris porcelain achieved international recognition at the 1851 London Crystal Palace Exhibition, one of the greatest nineteenth-century international fairs.

STYLE

The Paris decorators ornamented their wares in the French manner, with a liberal use of colored enamel and gilt. There was no attempt to cater to American tastes as the Limoges companies did.

The Paris factories specialized in dinner and dessert services. The quality is consistently fine. Many of the decorators had previously worked as artists or potters at Sevres.

Strewn flower sprigs, especially cornflowers, were often found on borders. Other favorite motifs were landscapes and medallions of Cupids. Parisian decorators did portrait and figure plates, and many were of outstanding quality.

Paris porcelain is easily distinguished from English porcelain of the same period. The Paris hard-paste body has a clear white translucence, the hand painting and gilding meticulously applied. The English porcelain of the period is bone china, slightly creamy in tone, and there is much less use of gilt and more restrained decoration.

MISCONCEPTIONS

Any unmarked porcelains in the rococo revival style are frequently sold as Old Paris by antique dealers today, even though the same style was produced in Limoges, Bohemia (now the Czech Republic), and Germany. Another misconception is that *Old Paris* refers to porcelain made from 1850 to 1890, when it actually includes porcelains made as early as the 1770s. Another error is that it refers to a specific factory. It is a term that includes about 37 factories and a number of firms that retailed Paris-decorated porcelain.

POPULAR PORCELAIN STUDIOS

Jacob Petit

Jacob Petit is one of the best-known Paris porcelain decorators. He was trained as a painter and traveled all over Europe visiting porcelain factories and decorating studios before opening up his own porcelain company in 1834 at Rue de Bondy in Paris. A few years later, he established a larger factory in Fontainebleu in which only ornamental articles were produced. He sold his company to one of his employees in 1862. Jacob Petit was a great designer and drew inspiration from many manufacturers and various periods. His products were quite ornamental and decorative.

Bloch — Porcelain de Paris

This decorating studio was begun at Rue de la Pierre-Leveé by Jean Marx Clauss in 1829. It went through several changes in management until the Achille Bloch family took over after 1900. The company is still in operation today producing luxury porcelain and expensive table services. Examples are found with hand-painted flowers and raised gold decoration. Famous artist L. Malpass decorated plates in an Oriental motif for this studio.

Feuillet & Boyer

Feuillet began a porcelain decorating studio at Rue de la Paix in 1820. Many of his blanks came from the Sevres factory. Feuillet was one of the best Paris decorators. He became partners with Boyer in 1834. Boyer was known for his exquisite flower painting, and he decorated many sets of plates with lifelike flower studies.

LeRosey

In 1856 LeRosey went into partnership with Paris decorator Louis Rihouet. Their studio was on Rue de la Paix. LeRosey was still working in 1900. He produced a series of beautiful plates with courting scenes and nymphs after Boucher. He also painted some exceptional portrait plates with raised gilt borders.

L'escalier de Cristal

Madame Desarneaux opened a porcelain-decorating studio at 38 Palais Royal around 1802. She also retailed crystal ware. She was succeeded by Boin in 1828, Bouvet in 1837, and Lahouche-Pannier from 1854 to 1900. The studio produced well-decorated portrait plates. F. Bellanger, an artist for this studio, did several plates with portraits of cavaliers in the Frans Hals style. Frans Hals (1582 – 1666) was the first great artist of the seventeenth century Dutch school and is regarded as one of the most talented of all portrait painters.

SARREGUEMINES

Utzschneider & Company purchased a failing factory in 1800 in Sarrgeumines, France. Utzschneider had worked at Wedgwood in England, and because of his artistic and technical expertise, gave the company new life and put Sarreguemines at the top of the industry. The company produced transfer-printed faience.

Soon after seeing Minton's display of majolica at the Paris Exhibition in 1855, Sarreguemines started its own line of majolica and showed the first pieces at the World Exposition in Paris in 1876. The company's majolica is of superb quality. The colors are vibrant and the glazes exceptional. The company also continued with its hand-painted faience pieces and produced some exceptional-quality chargers. The company is still in operation today.

SEVRES

Sevres is the luxury name in French porcelain. The earliest product, a soft-paste porcelain which was translucent and flawless, was first made in 1745 at Vincennes, under the blessing of Louis XV. By the early 1800s, only hard-paste porcelains were being made. The background colors were rich and exquisite. Bleu de roi, bleu turquoise, and rose pompadour were the company's most famous ground colors. The finest artists of the time decorated the elaborate cabinet plates with portrait, landscape, and floral reserves surrounded by panels of exquisite gilding.

A Sevres table service, ordered by Catherine II of Russia in 1776, was the first neoclassical service made by the factory. It contained 797 pieces. The plates have Catherine's monogram in the center, framed by a laurel wreath. The ground is turquoise (bleu celeste). Cameo heads, which reflect Catherine's interest in antique carved stones, are on the border.

In the last part of the eighteenth century, Sevres produced high-quality portraits on plates. They included the kings and queens of France and their families and members of the French court.

When Napoleon came to power in 1804, he inherited a series of royal residences and proceeded to furnish them as elegantly as possible. He became a welcome patron of the decorative arts and purchased lavish services from Sevres that often bore symbols suggestive of the empire, including classical and laurel leaf motifs.

Napoleon revived the tradition of ordering large table services for use as diplomatic gifts. Each service contained about 100 to 140 separate items, many of which were well-decorated plates. This tradition was continued through the first half of the nineteenth century.

One of the most famous sets of Sevres plates ever produced was presented by Louis-Phillippe to Metternich, the Austrian diplomat in 1823. These plates show the work of the Sevres factory, including sculptors and trimmers, the preparation of clay, and painters and gilders.

Sevres Manufactory, postcard, Edition Artistique C. M., Paris.

Many pieces of undecorated ware were sold at Sevres during the mid-to-late 1800s, often of inferior quality. These were decorated by companies and *hausmalers* (freelance painters) in France and abroad, sometimes with an intent to deceive the purchaser. Buyers should be aware that many items with Sevres marks were really decorated outside the company. The most common are portrait plates showing French royalty. These Sevres-style porcelain plates are not usually the quality of those painted at the Sevres factory, but they are still very attractive and well painted. They can certainly add to a decorative plate collection. Today most of the true Sevres porcelain items are in museums and royal and private collections.

Showroom at Sevres Manufactory, postcard, F. F., Paris.

Keller & Guérin, Luneville, France, c. 1880s. 8½"; pansy transfer. $50.00 – 65.00.

David Johnston, France, c. 1876. Creamware, 8⅛"; black and white transfer French battle scene. $100.00 – 125.00.

David Johnston, France, c. 1876. Creamware, 8½"; black and white transfer French battle scene. $100.00 – 125.00.

Limoges, J. Pouyet, c. 1891 – 1932, artist signed "Lefort." Charger, 13½"; dramatic hand-painted purple and white flowers on a dark turquoise and gold ground. $450.00 – 500.00. (See mark #63.)

Limoges, B & H and Coffe marks, c. 1891 – 1914. Scalloped charger, 12¼"; portrait of prince, maiden, and Cupid, heavy 2" gold border. $800.00 – 900.00.

Close-up.

Limoges, L. R. L. (Lazeyras, Rosenfeldt & Lehman), c. 1920s, artist signed. 10"; game plate with hand-painted seagulls, gold rococo border. $400.00 – 450.00. (See mark #64.)

Limoges, B & H (Blakeman & Henderson), c. 1890s, artist signed. Portrait charger, 12½", hand-painted lady with waist-length hair, roses, head of lioness in foreground, pierced for hanging. $1,000.00 – 1,200.00. (See mark #65.)

Close-up.

Limoges, T & V (Tressemann & Vogt), c. 1892 – 1907. 11"; Art Nouveau style, home decorated, profile of lady with leafy headband and head scarf, flowing blonde hair on a gold medallion, dark brown ground with garland of autumn leaves. $500.00 – 600.00. (See mark #66.)

Limoges, Borgfeldt, George, c. 1906 – 1920, artist signed. 10"; hand-painted apples and grapes, gold rococo border, pierced for hanging. $300.00 – 400.00. (See mark #67.)

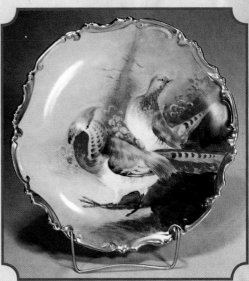

Limoges, L. R. L., c. 1920s, artist signed "Muville." Charger, 13¼"; hand-painted male and female game birds, pierced for hanging. $500.00 – 600.00.

Limoges, T & V, c. 1907 – 1919. Charger, 11½"; professionally decorated, roses and gold, rococo border. $400.00 – 500.00. (See mark #68.)

Limoges, B & H, c. 1890s. Scalloped, 10"; hand-painted swan in lake, green ground, professionally decorated. $300.00 – 350.00.

Limoges, Klingenberg & Dwenger decorating mark, c. 1900 – 1910. Molded-edged charger, 1½"; boy fishing in lake, mixed decoration. $350.00 – 400.00. (See mark #69.)

Limoges, L. R. L., signed "Duval." Charger, 16"; hand-painted fruit still life, gold rococo border. $500.00 – 600.00.

Limoges, Coiffe and Flambeau decorating mark, c. 1895, artist signed. Scalloped plate from fish service, 9½"; hand-painted fish swimming through underwater pink flowers on pale blue/yellow ground, gold trim. $125.00 – 150.00.

Limoges, T & V, c. 1907 – 1912. Charger, 12½"; hand-painted pink and purple clover blossoms on green border with white center, gold rococo border. $250.00 – 300.00. (See mark #71.)

Limoges, B & H, c. 1890s. 9¼"; half of unusual plate has ribbons of hand-painted daisies on black ground, other half has roses on pale green, lavish gilding. $250.00 – 300.00.

Limoges, Guerin, William, c. 1901, initialed and dated. Charger, 13½"; vivid purple flowers on pale green background, home decorated, pierced for hanging. $275.00 – 375.00. (See mark #72.)

Limoges, Pouyat, J., c. 1891, artist signed. Dubois. Plate, 9"; gold rococo border, hand-painted courting scene. $300.00 – 400.00.

Limoges, B & H, c. 1890s. 9¼"; professionally decorated morning glories and gilt. $150.00 – 200.00.

Limoges, Guerin, c. 1880 – 1891, artist signed. Charger, 12½"; family having tea, hand painted, flowers alternating with heavy gilt scrolls on border. $800.00 – 1,000.00.

Close-up.

Close-up of sailboats.

Limoges, L S & S (Straus, Lewis & Sons), c. 1890 – 1925. Plaque, 9½"; hand-painted flowers and scrolls, panel of sailboats. $200.00 – 250.00. (See mark #73.)

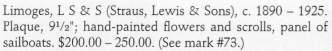

Limoges, G. Demartine & Cie, c. 1891 – 1900, artist signed "J. Soustre." 9¼"; beautifully painted portrait of Mrs. Sheridan after Gainsborough, cobalt and raised gold border. $1,000.00 – 1,200.00. (See mark #74.)

Close-up.

Limoges, GDA (Gerard, Dufraisseix & Abbot), c. 1900 – 1941. 9½"; border of green fern-like leaves, a band of pink, white and yellow flowers, gilt. $40.00 – 50.00. (See mark #75.)

Limoges, T & V (Tresseman & Vogt), c. 1907 – 1919, for Greenleaf & Crosby, artist signed. 9¼"; hand-painted orchids, marked "Stanhopea Mariana" on back, heavy gilt on green border. $250.00 – 300.00.

Limoges, Haviland, c. 1893 – 1930, artist signed "M. Smith." 8¼"; portrait of woman with long hair, probably amateur artist, red and gilt scrolls on border. $150.00 – 175.00. (See mark #76.)

Limoges, William Guerin, c. 1891 – 1900. Cake plate, 11"; garlands of hand-painted roses with intricate gold design on border. $300.00 – 350.00.

Limoges, Haviland, c. 1880s, made for Tiffany, NY. 9"; mixed decoration of fruit, 1½" gold border. $75.00 – 100.00. (See mark #77.)

Limoges, Haviland, c. 1880s, made for Tiffany, NY. 9"; mixed decoration of fruit, 1½" gold border. $75.00 – 100.00.

Limoges, Haviland, c. 1880s, made for Tiffany, NY. 9"; mixed decoration of fruit, 1½" gold border. $75.00 – 100.00.

Limoges, R. Delinieres, c. 1900, made special for 1900 exhibition in Paris, artist signed "Prosper.", 10"; rare plate with purple monochrome and white decoration, bird in center with just the image of babies in a nest, cobalt blue border with lush gold paste and beaded decoration. $600.00 – 700.00. (See mark #78.)

Close-up.

Limoges, unidentified maker, made for A. Schmidt & Sons, NY, c. 1920s. 8⅓" each; heavy gold border, three large roses and gold leaves on each. $150.00 – 200.00.

Limoges, T & V, c. 1892 – 1907. 8¼"; mixed decoration, game birds in natural settings, yellow roses and gold on border. $50.00 – 75.00. (See mark #79.)

Limoges, T & V, c. 1892 – 1907. 8¼"; mixed decoration, game birds in natural settings, yellow roses and gold on border. $50.00 – 75.00.

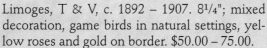

Limoges, T & V, c. 1892 – 1907. 8¼"; mixed decoration, game birds in natural settings, yellow roses and gold on border. $50.00 – 75.00.

Limoges, T & V, c. 1892 – 1907. 8¼"; mixed decoration, game birds in natural settings, yellow roses and gold on border. $50.00 – 75.00.

Limoges, GDA, c. 1900 – 1941. Scalloped, 8¹⁄₃"; mixed decoration with array of roses in center, cobalt blue and gold borders. $100.00 – 125.00. (See mark #80.)

Limoges, Haviland, c. 1876 – 1880, artist signed "Barharin." 9¼"; hand-painted pomegranates, coral dotted with gold and white daisies on border. $150.00 – 200.00. (See mark #81.)

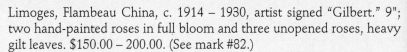

Limoges, Flambeau China, c. 1914 – 1930, artist signed "Gilbert." 9"; two hand-painted roses in full bloom and three unopened roses, heavy gilt leaves. $150.00 – 200.00. (See mark #82.)

Limoges, Union Ceramique, c. 1900 – 1938, made special for Reizenstein Sons, Pittsburgh, Pennsylvania. Service plate, 10³⁄₄"; over-painted roses with lavish gold paste roses, swirls and beading. $100.00 – 125.00. (See mark #83.)

Limoges, Raynaud, M., c. 1900, after Stieler. 9½"; exceptional painting of Anna Hillmayr. $500.00 – 550.00. (See mark #85.)

Close-up.

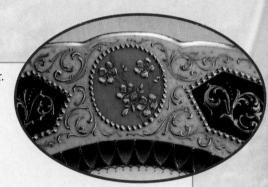

Close-up of border.

Limoges, Haviland, c. 1893 – 1920. 9"; hand-painted portrait of lady with a floral hat, heavy gold medallions with flowers and scrolls on border. $400.00 – 500.00.

Limoges, Haviland, c. 1893 – 1920. 9"; hand-painted portrait of lady with a ruffled hat and collar, heavy gold medallions with birds and scrolls on border. $400.00 – 500.00.

Close-up.

Limoges, Haviland, Charles Field, c. 1882 – 1900. Wavy-form oyster plate, 7$\frac{1}{3}$"; blue flowers and brown leaves. $150.00 – 175.00. (See mark #86.)

Limoges, Haviland, Charles Field, c. 1882 – 1900. Wavy-form oyster plate, 7$\frac{1}{3}$"; pink flowers and brown leaves. $150.00 – 175.00.

Limoges, Haviland, Charles Field, c. 1882 – 1900. Wavy-form oyster plate, 7¹/₃"; purple flowers and brown leaves. $150.00 – 175.00.

Limoges, J. Pouyat, c. 1876 – 1890. 8¹/₃"; hand-painted portrait of girl with long brown hair, cobalt and gilt. $150.00 – 200.00.

Limoges, Gerard, Dufrasisseix & Abbot, c. 1900, artist signed "Laraque." 7¹/₂"; well-painted portrait of baby, pink border with gold flowers. $300.00 – 350.00.

Close-up.

Close-up.

Limoges, Gerard, Dufrasisseix & Abbot, c. 1900, artist signed "Laraque." 7¹/₂"; well-painted portrait of little girl, pink border with gold flowers. $300.00 – 350.00.

Limoges, Gerard, Dufrasisseix & Abbot, c. 1900, artist signed "Laraque." 7¹/₂"; well-painted portrait of little girl, pink border with gold flowers. $300.00 – 350.00.

Close-up.

Close-up.

Limoges, Gerard, Dufrasisseix & Abbot, c. 1900, artist signed "Laraque." 7¹/₂"; well-painted portrait of little girl, pink border with gold flowers. $300.00 – 350.00.

Limoges, Flambeau China, c. 1890 – 1905, artist signed Duca. Fish set including platter, 12 plates, and serving bowl with underplate; hand-painted fish swimming among flowering branches, peach shaded to yellow ground, gilt braided border. $2,500.00 – 3,000.00.

Plate from fish set.

Plate from fish set.

Plate from fish set.

Close-up of fish.

Haviland, c. 1960s. Scalloped, $9^5/8$"; collector reproduction of White House historical plate made for Abraham Lincoln, originally made in 1861. $50.00 – 75.00.

Haviland, Limoges, c. 1876 – 1880. 10¼"; hand-painted portrait of lady with unusual hat, painted outside factory. $700.00 – 800.00.

Close-up.

Limoges, W. Guerin & Co., c. 1900 – 1932. Scalloped plate, 9"; professional decoration of hunting dog gazing at birds, gold etched rim. $300.00 – 350.00. (See mark #87.)

Limoges, Comte D'Artoise, c. 1930s, artist signed "Leon." 9"; hand-painted purple and white flowers with heavy gold border. $200.00 – 250.00.

Limoges, Royal China, c. 1900 – 1920, artist signed "J. Soustre." Charger, 11"; lush pink and purple roses in foreground, castle scene with lake and forest setting in background. $400.00 – 500.00.

Limoges, W. Guerin & Co., c. 1900 – 1932, artist signed. Charger, 11"; two hand-painted game birds, rococo gold border. $400.00 – 500.00.

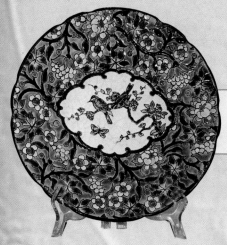

Longwy, France, c. 1878 – 1920. Art pottery plate, 7¼"; cloisonné-style decoration, bird and flowers. $175.00 – 200.00.

Longwy, France, c. 1878 – 1920. Art pottery plate, 7¼"; cloisonné-style floral decoration. $175.00 – 200.00.

Longwy, France, c. 1878 – 1920. Art pottery plate, 7¼"; cloisonné-style floral decoration. $175.00 – 200.00.

Longwy, France, c. 1875 – 1900. Art pottery plate, 9¾"; cloisonné effect, hand-painted birds in center. $250.00 – 300.00.

Longwy, France, c. 1875 – 1900. Art pottery plate, 9¾"; hand-painted birds in center, floral border. $200.00 – 250.00.

Limoges, J. Pouyat blank, decorated Etienne, J. Fils, Paris, c. 1876 – 1890, artist signed "A. Faugeron." 10"; cobalt blue border with hand gilding, well-painted courting scene with a dog. $500.00 – 600.00. (See mark #104.)

Close-up.

Paris, c. 1840 – 1850, unmarked. 9½"; center medallion of hand-painted flowers, gilt decoration on border. $300.00 – 350.00.

Paris, Paul Blot Studio, c. 1850s, artist signed "L. Malpass." 8½"; spectacular border with heavy gold paste butterfly, bamboo, Mt. Fuji, swan, and exotic bird, portrait of an Asian lady with a parasol, artist also worked at Minton. $900.00 – 1,000.00. (See mark #105.)

Close-up.

Paris, Paul Blot Studio, c. 1850s, artist signed "L. Malpass." 8½"; spectacular border with heavy gold paste winged snake, butterfly, peonies, Mt. Fuji, and exotic bird; portrait of an Asian man holding a fan, artist also worked at Minton. $900.00 – 1,000.00.

Paris, Lehoche-Pannier, c. 1854 – 1900. 9½"; hand-painted portrait of Madame Maintenon, framework of white roses on border. $700.00 – 800.00. (See mark #106.)

Close-up.

Etienne & Fils Studio, Paris, c. 1890 – 1920, artist signed J. Pascault. 9⅔"; hand-painted courting scene in center, heavy etched gold border. $200.00 – 250.00. (See mark #107.)

Close-up.

Sevres style, decorated in Paris studio, c. 1830s. Dish, 9¼"; painted in style of Fallot, a Sevres artist in 1773 – 1790, cobalt border with French enameling and gilt scrolling, intricate arabesque painting of fruit, flowers, cupids, and dragons in center. $500.00 – 550.00.

Sevres style, decorated in Paris studio, c. 1870s. 10"; hand-painted portrait of Louis de Bourbon, intricate Sevres blue border with two cupids on top. $600.00 – 700.00.

Close-up of portrait.

Close-up of border.

Jacob Petit, Paris, c. 1840 – 1850s, signed "J. P." 10"; ornate Capodimonte border with six hand-painted allegorical medallions. $2,000.00 – 2,500.00. (See mark #108.)

Sevres style, c. 1890s, signed "E. Sieffert de Sevres." 9½"; hand-painted little girl holding an alphabet book, cobalt border with gold paste scroll decoration. $750.00 – 850.00. (See mark #109.)

Close-up.

Sevres style, Paris decorating studio, c. 1900. 9¼"; center medallion of military scene at Conti. $300.00 – 350.00.

Sevres style, Paris decorating studio, c. 1890, artist signed. 9½"; hand-painted portrait of lady, floral medallions on aqua, gold scrollwork. $300.00 – 350.00.

Sevres style, Lerosey Studio, Paris, c. 1890s, signed "E. Sieffert." 9"; portrait of Marie Antoinette, raised gold decoration on border, some gilt wear. $450.00 – 550.00. (See mark #110.)

Sevres style, Paris decorating studio, c. 1890. 9½"; hand-painted portrait of Marie Antoinette, hand-painted flowers on cream, gold enameling on pink. $300.00 – 350.00.

Sevres style, Paris decorating studio, c. 1883. 8¾"; portrays woman in a flowing dress with blue ruffles, faint outline of dressing table in background, signed by Sevres artist Eugene Sieffert. $800.00 – 900.00.

Close-up.

Sevres style, Paris decorating studio, c. 1883. 8³/₄"; hand painting of "La Fontaine d'amour" after Fragonard, cobalt blue band and heavy gilt scrolling on border. $800.00 – 900.00.

Sevres style, Paris decorating studio, c. 1868 – 1880. 8³/₄"; array of hand-painted flowers, gold design on border. $100.00 – 125.00. (See mark #111.)

Sevres style, Paris decorating studio, c. 1870 – 1890s. 9⁷/₈"; armorial plate with blue border, raised gold roses. $500.00 – 600.00. (See mark #112.)

Close-up.

Sevres style, Paris decorating studio, c. 1870 – 1890s. 9⁷/₈"; three bands of royal blue with raised gilt decoration on border, hand-painted flower basket in center, nine cartouches of flowers framed with gold beads or leaves. $300.00 – 350.00.

Sevres style, Paris decorating studio, c. 1880 – 1890. 9¼"; cobalt borders with gilt, hand-painted portrait of French court beauty in center. $300.00 – 350.00. (See mark #113.)

Sevres style, Paris decorating studio, c. 1880 – 1890. 9¼"; cobalt borders with gilt, hand-painted portrait of French court beauty in center. $300.00 – 350.00.

Sevres style, Paris decorating studio, c. 1880 – 1890. 9¼"; cobalt borders with gilt, hand-painted portrait of French court beauty in center. $300.00 – 350.00.

Close-up.

Escalier de Cristal Studio, Paris, c. 1890s, Minton blank, artist signed "F. Bellanger." 9¹⁄₃"; hand-painted portrait of cavalier in the Franz Hals style, gold etched border. $500.00 – 600.00.

Close-up.

Escalier de Cristal Studio, Paris, c. 1890s, Minton blank, artist signed "F. Bellanger." 9¹⁄₃"; hand-painted portrait of cavalier playing mandolin in the Franz Hals style, gold etched border. $500.00 – 600.00. (See mark #114.)

Close-up.

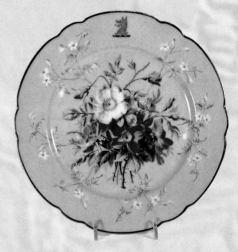

Close-up of flowers.

Boyer Studio, Paris, c. 1845 – 1850. 9$\frac{1}{3}$"; exquisite flower painting, gold dragon crest, violet pink ground. $400.00 – 500.00. (See mark #115.)

Boyer Studio, Paris, c. 1845 – 1850. 9$\frac{1}{3}$"; exquisite flower painting, gold dragon crest, violet pink ground. $400.00 – 500.00.

Boyer Studio, Paris, c. 1845 – 1850. 9$\frac{1}{3}$"; exquisite flower painting, gold dragon crest, violet pink ground. $400.00 – 500.00.

LaRoche, Palais Royal, Paris, c. 1840s. 9¹/₂"; hand-painted portrait of Louis XIII framed by gold leaves, pink border. $350.00 – 400.00. (See mark #116.)

Close-up.

Close-up.

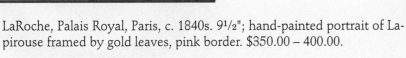

LaRoche, Palais Royal, Paris, c. 1840s. 9¹/₂"; hand-painted portrait of Lapirouse framed by gold leaves, pink border. $350.00 – 400.00.

Puchet Deroche, Paris, c. 1830 – 1850. 8³/₄"; hand-painted pastoral scene woman milking goat, man carrying a basket, cobalt border, medallions of flowers, excellent gilt work. $300.00 – 350.00. (See mark #117.)

Boyer, Feuillet Studio, Paris, c. 1834 – 1855. 9½"; cobalt and gold cobblestone border, well-painted flowers in center. $400.00 – 450.00. (See mark #118.)

Boyer, Feuillet Studio, Paris, c. 1834 – 1855. 9½"; cobalt and gold cobblestone border, well-painted flowers in center. $400.00 – 450.00.

Boyer, Feuillet Studio, Paris, c. 1834 – 1855. 9½"; cobalt and gold cobblestone border, well-painted flowers in center. $400.00 – 450.00.

Unmarked, probably Paris, c. 1860s, artist signed "P. Amaury." Earthenware charger, 13⅓"; hand-painted portrait of a young girl with feathered hat and curls. $300.00 – 350.00.

Lerosey, Paris, c. 1880s. 9½"; hand-painted courting scene, pale blue border with gilt. $400.00 – 450.00.

Lerosey, Paris, c. 1880s. 9½"; well-painted portrait of young lady with black hair and dressed in black lace, elaborate raised gold border. $1,000.00 – 1,200.00. (See mark #119.)

Close-up of portrait.

Close-up of border.

Paris studio, unidentified mark, c. 1870. 10⅛"; hand-painted Asian man looking through a telescope, gold stars and bird in background, attributed to L. Malpass, turquoise and gold reticulated border. $500.00 – 600.00. (See mark #120.)

Close-up.

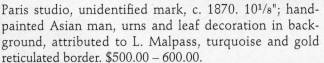

Close-up of border.

Paris studio, unidentified mark, c. 1870. 10⅛"; hand-painted Asian man, urns and leaf decoration in background, attributed to L. Malpass, turquoise and gold reticulated border. $500.00 – 600.00.

Unmarked, Paris, c. 1890s, artist signed "F. Roche." Bread plate, 10" x 9½"; exquisite flower and butterfly painting, blue turned-over edges. $400.00 – 450.00.

Close-up.

Close-up.

Sevres, c. 1780s, artist signed "LeGuay." 9½"; rich gros blue ground with intricate pattern of jeweling and gilt. $1,200.00 – 1,500.00. (See mark #140.)

Sevres, c. 1780. Soft-paste porcelain, 9¹/₃"; hand-painted castle and lake scene, Rose Pompadour border, jeweling and gilt decoration. $1,200.00 – 1,400.00.

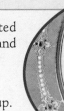

Close-up.

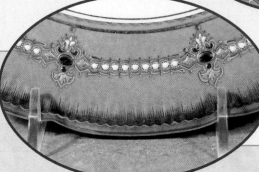

Close-up of border.

Sarreguemines, c. 1870s. Faience charger, 14"; hand-painted nanny holding baby, parents and friend looking on, castle in background. $600.00 – 700.00.

Sarreguemines, c. 1870s. Faience charger, 14";
hand-painted wedding scene, castle in background.
$600.00 – 700.00.

Close-up.

French Faience, unknown maker, artist signed "Dannus." Charger, 14½";
portrait of lovely young woman. $600.00 – 800.00.

Unmarked, probably French. Scalloped, 8½"; hand-
painted butterflies and birds. $100.00 – 125.00.

Unmarked, French, c. 1900 – 1920, artist signed "Amelie." Square, 8½"; hand-painted birds painted on a diagonal. $75.00 – 100.00.

Unmarked, French, c. 1900 – 1920, artist signed "Amelie." Square, 8½"; hand-painted birds painted on a diagonal. $75.00 – 100.00.

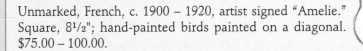

Unmarked, French, c. 1900 – 1920, artist signed "Amelie." Square, 8½"; hand-painted birds painted on a diagonal. $75.00 – 100.00.

Unmarked, French, c. 1900 – 1920, artist signed "Amelie." Square, 8½"; hand-painted birds painted on a diagonal. $75.00 – 100.00.

Since Meissen developed hard-paste porcelain in 1708, Germany has been one of the centers of porcelain production in Europe. Some of the best examples of hand-painted cabinet plates were produced by Meissen, KPM, and the Dresden studios.

Also, in the nineteenth century hundreds of porcelain manufacturers began operating in Bavaria and Saxony.

Kaolin (china clay) was abundant, as was inexpensive coal for firing the kilns. From the late 1800s through 1930, Germany produced most American souvenir plates. Decorated with scenes of small-town America, some were even hand painted. They were often made either for merchants to promote their businesses or to commemorate carnivals, fairs, and special events.

DRESDEN PORCELAIN DECORATING STUDIOS

At the end of the eighteenth century, the Romantic movement influenced all areas of intellectual life in Germany. One of the centers of this movement was Dresden. Artists, poets, musicians, and philosophers were attracted by the Baroque beauty of the city, with its splendid collections, its charming surroundings, and the stimulating intellectual and artistic atmosphere, and moved there. Important artists made Dresden a center of the Romantic school of painting.

In the late nineteenth century, there was a considerable demand among the middle classes for porcelain and other handcrafted objects for interior decoration at moderate prices. This demand was met by the Dresden decorating studios.

City of Dresden, postcard, #6003 Hermann, Dresden.

Directories from 1855 to 1944 show more than 200 painting shops in Dresden alone. Most of them employed several artists. Many shops also contracted with decorators who worked at home and were paid by the piece.

Many of the large shops had their studios near the Dresden Main-Railway Station at Prager and Zinzendor-

fer Streets. Many of the shops dealt in antiques and fine art, and some had their own kilns.

Large quantities of white porcelain pieces, or blanks, were bought from porcelain manufacturers in Germany, Austria, and Limoges, France, by the Dresden studios for decorating and marketing throughout the world as Dresden china. Much of the whiteware was ordered without marks, and the decorators put on their own marks. Because the demand for Dresden porcelains was so great, the studios sometimes had to use blanks that were already marked. The decorators hid those marks under blobs of gold paint or under gold flower blossoms. The size and shape of a blossom depended on the size and shape of the original porcelain manufacturer's mark. A Dresden style came into being that was a mixture of Meissen and Vienna flower and figure painting.

FRANZISKA HIRSCH

Franziska Hirsch operated a porcelain studio on Struwestrasse 19 in Dresden from 1894 to 1930. It decorated in the Meissen and Vienna styles. The company's early marks were variations of crossed lines, or staffs, and the initial H in overglaze blue.

In 1896, Meissen successfully won a lawsuit against Hirsch's use of the two crossed staffs with "H." A new mark of a stylized H with wings and "Dresden" were then used by Hirsch.

Hirsch used blanks by Meissen, Rosenthal, and MZ Austria and used the gold overglaze flower to hide the manufacturers' marks. The favorite decorative styles used by Hirsch were Dresden flowers in bouquets or star garlands on pristine white grounds with gilt borders. Hirsch had a staff of talented flower painters.

Hirsch also produced a few museum-quality cabinet plates. Examples can be found with a burgundy luster, or "Tiffany glaze." Heavy gold paste work, beads, and pearl jeweling were used to enhance the plates.

RICHARD KLEMM

Karl Richard Klemm had a decorating studio on Vorstadt Striesen in Dresden from around 1869 to 1949. Klemm was an outstanding artist in his own right and was known for painting in the Meissen and Vienna styles.

A number of trademarks were used by Richard Klemm. His studio was part of the cooperative using the crown Dresden mark in 1883. The cooperative also included Donath & Co., Oswald Lorenz, and Adolph Hamann.

Apart from the group crown Dresden mark, Klemm also used a monogram mark consisting of a reversed *R* joined to a *K* under a crown with "Dresden" below. Klemm also used "Dresden" under a star or asterisk, a mark also used by several other decorators. As recently as 1940, Klemm lost a lawsuit to Meissen for misuse of a sword mark.

The Richard Klemm studio produced a tremendous output of porcelain and made some of the best and, unfortunately, some of the worst. Quality depended on the skill of the painter and who ordered the pieces.

Blanks commonly used were by Meissen, Rosenthal, KPM, Silesia Porcelain Factory, and Limoges. Klemm painted Watteau courting scenes alternating with florals made popular by Helena Wolfsohn in the nineteenth

Portrait of beautiful woman, entitled La Crucle Cassee, J. B. Greuze, postcard, Stengel & Co., Dresden 29897.

century. Popular colors used were apple green, black, pink, yellow, and blue. The studio also had a brisk business in dinner services with "Dresden flowers" and gilt.

Klemm produced some top-quality work for important clients that easily rivaled that of Meissen. The company decorated cabinet plates and plaques with heavy paste work. Some examples are plates and trays having insets with excellent figure painting and gold fretwork. Top artists were N. Kiesel, A. Bock, and J. Wagner. Klemm's studio did the decoration for a number of KPM plaques. One recently sold on an Internet auction for $7,626.00. It was a lovely portrait of Clementine, signed "V. L. Schinzel."

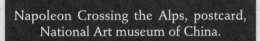

Napoleon Crossing the Alps, postcard, National Art museum of China.

AMBROSIUS LAMM

Ambrosius Lamm operated a porcelain painting studio and arts and antique shop from 1887 to 1949. It was located at Zinzendorfstrasse 28 in Dresden. He had approximately 25 employees by 1894, which grew to about 40 in 1907. In 1928 Rudolf Pitschke was proprietor.

Lamm's studio is known for painting in the Meissen, Vienna, and Copenhagen styles. According to an 1906 issue of *Keramadressbuch*, Lamm's specialties were "Old Dresden Flowers, Watteau and mythology, decorated luxury and utility articles in the old and new style." Lamm bought blanks from a number of manufacturing firms, including Meissen, Rosenthal, Hutschenreuther, and Silesia.

At least three different marks were used by Lamm, including a pensive angel with "Dresden and Saxony," "L" within a shield, and the most common mark, a painting of a lamb with "Dresden" underneath. He apparently attempted to use a crossed swords mark as well, because Meissen took action against him in 1943.

The Lamm studio consistently produced work of outstanding quality. Lamm decorated cabinet plates rivaling the quality of Royal Vienna and Sevres. His portrait plates were exceptional. He enjoyed painting historical figures, such as Napoleon, as well as beautiful women and cherubs. Many examples can be found with cherubs holding fruit or flowers or playing musical instruments. Cherubs were often portrayed among fluffy clouds.

The borders on Lamm's cabinet plates were often a rich cobalt blue. Lamm was a master of gilding and heavy paste decoration. Artists working for Lamm were S. Lieb, O. Dietrich, and Danner.

Lamm produced a series of game plates. The studio took special orders to decorate dinner and service plates for wealthy customers. Today, sets can be found with monograms on the centers or borders of the plates.

Cupid with doves postcard, B. W. 309, Germany.

CARL THIEME

Carl Thieme was possibly one of the best copycats of Meissen porcelain. He started a china-decorating studio in Potschappel, Germany, in 1867. The town is located in eastern Germany in the state of Saxony, between the foothills of the Erzgebirge Mountains and 10 miles from Dresden. In 1921, the town was combined with the villages of Deuben and Doehlen to form the city of Freital.

Thieme's studio decorated porcelain whiteware it bought from the C. G. Schierholz factory in Plaue, Saxony, in the Meissen and Vienna styles. On October 2, 1872, the company began producing its own porcelain and was named Saxon Porcelain Manufactory Dresden. One of the frequently used marks from 1888 to 1901 was crossed lines with a *T* in underglaze or overglaze blue or black.

The company openly copied Meissen, Vienna, and Sevres forms, figures, and decoration. There were many quarrels between the Meissen and Thieme companies, some of them taken to court. Thieme's early mark, various forms of crossed lines with the letter *T*, was

Marie Antoinette, postcard #B202.

criticized by Meissen, who thought it was too close to its own famous crossed swords mark. Thieme promised not to use it and declared its intention to mark its porcelain with "S.P.F." (for Saxonian Porcelain Factory) in script, which it did in 1901. It included "Dresden" below the letters, as the "Dresden" and "Dresden china" were not protected.

Carl Thieme produced beautiful dessert sets with hand-painted flowers and gilt with reticulated borders. His Marie Antoinette plates with the "M A" monogram are popular with collectors today.

RICHARD WEHSNER

Richard Wehsner ran a porcelain studio at Zinzendorfstrasse 16 in Dresden from 1895 to 1956. The company produced finely painted Meissen-type decoration for export. Its flower painting was outstanding, and a number of portrait and allegorical plates were decorated with beaded and jeweled borders.

HELENA WOLFSOHN

The earliest Dresden studio to copy Meissen's designs was Helena Wolfsohn, which began operation in 1843. During the period between 1875 and 1915, there were 30 painters working at the studio. After Helena Wolfsohn's death, the business was continued by her daughter, Madame Elb, and then by her son. In 1919 Walter Ernst Stephan took over, but little is known of the late production.

Helena Wolfsohn used various forms of "A R" in script from 1843 to 1883. In 1879, Meissen took Wolfsohn to court regarding the use of the "A R" mark. Wolfsohn won, and Meissen appealed. The ruling was overturned in 1881. At that time, the firm adopted a mark using a crown with the letter *D* underneath. Wolfsohn also used "Dresden," surmounted by a crown. The gold overglaze flower mark was used from 1880 to 1945 to cover the manufacturer's mark.

Wolfsohn purchased white china blanks from the Meissen factory and had them decorated by her own staff of painters and gilders. The workshop of Helena Wolfsohn was one of the most prolific decorating studios in Dresden. It specialized in painting vases and tea and coffee wares. The decoration was typically divided into quarters, with figures decorated in the Watteau style alternating with flowers on rich ground colors.

Dessert services were painted in the Meissen style with fruit, birds, landscapes, and sea views. Plates often had reticulated or basket-weave borders. Wolfsohn produced some portrait plates with Tiffany luster borders.

 ## HUTSCHENREUTHER

The C. M. (Carl Magnus) Hutschenreuther Porcelain Factory began operation in Bavaria in 1814. Carl's son, Lorenz, established the first china factory in Selb, Germany, in 1857. While the early German factories, such as Meissen and KPM, produced porcelain for the courts and the aristocracy, private factories such as Hutschenreuther made china available to the general public.

In 1918, Hutschenreuther took over the important co-op decorating shops of Richard Klemm, Donath & Co., and O. Lorenz, which had already been supplied with Hutschenreuther blanks. It established the art department of C. M. Hutschenreuther in Dresden. Top-quality cabinet portrait plates after famous eighteenth century artists in the Dresden museum were made.

Hutschenreuther is still in business today, producing limited edition plates, figures, and dinnerware. One of its best-known dinnerware patterns is Blue Onion.

 ## KPM

Frederick the Great, whose passion was white gold, gave KPM (King's Porcelain Manufactory) its name and trademark, the royal blue scepter, in 1763. The company is located in Berlin, Germany, and is one of the top porcelain companies in the world. It is still in operation today.

KPM is especially known for its finely decorated dessert services. Cupids, Watteau paintings, battle scenes, historical scenes, and landscapes have been done with great skill. Of particular importance is KPM's realistic flower and fruit painting. Each flower or piece of fruit is meticulously painted by hand, and most works are personally initialed by the painter. Many have heavy gold paste embellishments surrounding the floral cartouche.

In the early twentieth century, KPM produced a set of cabinet plates to honor the wives of American presidents from Mrs. George Washington through Mrs. Woodrow Wilson. They are 10½" with gold borders, and each has an American eagle at the top, flags at each side, and a name plate inscribed at the bottom. S. Wagner, a celebrated porcelain artist of Berlin and Vienna, was the artist.

There have been many imitations of KPM's scepter mark. The Kranichfeld Company, around 1903, had what looks like a scepter with a flame and ".KPM." as its trademark. Paul Muller, Selb, 1890, used a scepter and "S." The most common mark confused with Berlin today is "KPM" with a vertical line on top. This mark has been used by Krister Porcelain, Waldenburg, Germany, in various forms since 1885.

MEISSEN

City of Meissen with view of Albrechtsburg, postcard, 910 Bruck & Sons, Meissen.

The first European porcelain company, Meissen, was established by King Augustus II. Beautiful cabinetware sets were produced as early as the 1700s. One of the most elaborate early sets was the Swan Service ordered by Count Bruhl in 1737. The entire surface of each piece was modeled in low relief with animals and water plants. The Swan Service is still being produced today. A single plate retails for $600.00 – 800.00.

The Japanese service commissioned by the Prussian King Frederick the Great in 1762 was decorated with wild animals reflecting the popular sport of hunting. The shape of the plates was derived from French silver.

Meissen painter Johann George Heintz was much admired for his outstanding European landscapes, which were based on Dutch engravings. The style gained popularity in the 1730s, and soon the painting of harbor scenes, landscapes, and battles achieved great popularity.

Meissen artists began to transfer the paintings in the famous Semper Gallery in Dresden, Germany, on to porcelain around 1800. Paintings by Angelica Kaufmann, Giovanni Antonio Canaletto, and other favorite Dutch and Italian artists were copied onto porcelain. Canaletto (1697 – 1768) was an Italian painter known for his sparkling views of Venice, Dresden, and other cities in Europe. Topographical plates from the Wellington service (1818 – 1820) had views of Dresden with magnificent gold borders.

Meissen decorated portrait plates, and these are rare and quite valuable today. The face of a beautiful woman was a common subject, although famous men were often used as well, such as Augustus II and Napoleon. This type of decoration was very expensive to produce, as it was only done by the top Meissen portrait artists. At the end of the eighteenth century, there was an increased demand by the wealthy for portrait items. Johann George Loehnig (1745 – 1806) was a famous Meissen portrait painter.

Meissen has produced a number of ornate cabinet plates and chargers that often have a rich cobalt ground with elaborate gilding. These chargers are often in a grape-leaf pattern, and the centers have hand-painted flowers or fruit.

Meissen produced many exquisite dinner sets with hand-painted flowers. Meissen flowers are stylized versions of well-known garden flowers (*deutsche blumen*) adapted to the decoration of porcelain. During the 1930s, many dinnerware sets of Meissen's Rose pattern were exported to the United States. The demand was so great for this pattern that many sets were decorated out of the factory and have strike marks to indicate outside painting. Another popular pattern is the Full Green Vine Wreath, and plates in this design can be found.

The oldest Meissen tableware decorations were its East Indian patterns with stylized sectionalized paintings of Oriental animals, flowers, and landscapes. Today the painters of East Indian designs have a selection of 160 colors and many different patterns, such as Purple Indian and the popular Dragon. Meissen plates with Oriental patterns are always top quality and prized by collectors.

Meissen's Blue Onion pattern has endured for over 250 years and is Meissen's best-known pattern. It has been copied by more companies than any other ceramic pattern in history. Many collectors agree that a piece of Blue Onion made by Meissen stands apart from its competitors. This is due to the meticulous handwork by which each piece is made and decorated.

In 1710, King Augustus II demanded that his new porcelain company produce blue underglaze decorations like those of the Chinese. The Blue Onion pattern was created in 1739 after Horoldt had perfected the blue underglaze paint. The model for the onion pattern was probably a flat bowl from the Chinese K'ang Hsi period (1662 – 1722), which is now displayed at the Meissen Museum.

The fruits are not onions, but were made to resemble Chinese peaches and pomegranates. The flower in the design is a cross between a peony and a chrysanthemum. The elements in the center of the pattern are bamboo (trunk, blossom, and leaves).

The original pattern of 1739 underwent a few changes. At first all the fruits on the border pointed inward, with the stems on the edge. After a few years, the arrangement changed. The fruits began to point alternately inward and outward.

The heads of the Meissen manufactory liked the pattern because it was cheaper to produce than other decorated wares. It could be painted by lower-paid "blue painters" and even by journeymen and apprentices. Also, it did not need the third firing that was necessary to fix enamel decoration, and no gilding was added to the standard ware.

During Victorian times, when home furnishing became darker and heavier, the onion pattern seemed to complement this new elaborate furniture style preferred by the wealthy middle class. After 1865, the Blue Onion pattern became a craze. Today in the Meissen manufactory, the onion pattern, as it always has been, is still hand painted.

Meissen's Blue Onion pattern has been widely copied by more than 60 European, American, and Oriental factories. Since the pattern wasn't copyrighted, it could be used by anyone. To protect the actual Meissen pieces, the company put the famous blue crossed swords mark at the foot of the bamboo trunk in the design in 1888. Meissen Blue Onion pieces without this mark date before 1888.

Meissen Blue Onion display, postcard courtesy of Meissen.

NYMPHENBURG

Prince Elector Max Joseph II of Bavaria's ruling Wittelsbach family was envious of the Meissen factory of King Augustus II. In 1747 he established a royal porcelain manufactory in an unused hunting lodge at Au, a town close to Munich. The factory became profitable and soon outgrew the hunting lodge. It was moved to Nymphenburg, where it remains today.

The company produced some lovely cabinet plates. In 1810, Prince Ludwig I commissioned a large table service with plates to be painted with copies of the most outstanding works in the Dresden gallery. Ludwig took

a great interest in the factory and promoted the painting department to the status of Art Institute.

During the period from 1842 through 1845 the Art Institute decorated two sets of plates, one of them celebrating, on porcelain, the Bavarian landscape, and the other consisting of a series of portraits of women in national costume. A plate from either of these services would be a prize for a collector.

Today many Nymphenburg cabinet sets can be found with realistic hand-painted flowers on pristine white or cobalt grounds.

ROSENTHAL

Philip Rosenthal operated a porcelain factory in Selb, Germany, in 1879, producing fine dinnerware, decorative items, and figures. The high-quality workmanship and simplicity of design made Rosenthal's dinnerware highly acclaimed, and much was exported to the United States. Collectors look for early patterns with hand painting and intricate molds. Single plates from luxury dinnerware services often make up parts of plate collections.

ROYAL BAYREUTH

The Royal Bayreuth company has a long history, beginning in 1794. It operated under the name Porcelain Factory Tettau from 1902 until 1957. In 1957, the company adopted the name Royally Privileged Porcelain Factory Tettau GMBH, which it still uses today. Today the firm produces dinnerware and limited-edition collectibles. Plates having the Rose Tapestry pattern or Sun Bonnet decorations are popular with collectors.

SCHLEGELMILCH BROTHERS

Two brothers, Erdmann and Reinhold Schlegelmilch, founded separate porcelain factories located in the Germanic region generally known as Prussia prior to World War I. Reinhold produced R. S. Prussia art porcelain. R. S. Prussia plates are highly sought after by collectors because of the intricate mold shapes and the wide variety of different decorations. The molds are ornately molded, or rococo, with scrolls and flowers as part of the designs. Many R. S. Prussia plates were decorated with transfer designs and were decorated over the glaze, as this was a less expensive method of decoration.

The Erdmann Schlegelmilch Company in Suhl, Germany, operated from 1881 to 1938 making household, table, and decorative porcelain. Many E. S. Germany pieces are decorated with classical or mythological themes. Some of the transfer decorations used on plates by E. S. Germany were based on paintings by Angelica Kauffman, an eighteenth century Swiss artist who worked primarily in a neoclassical style.

SCHUMANN

Heinrich Schumann founded this factory in 1881 in Arzburg, Bavaria, and the company is still in operation today. It produces decorative porcelain, dinnerware services, gift articles, and fancy coffee and tea sets, and its pieces are very popular with collectors today. Its best-known patterns have the Dresden Flowers motif and are named Empress, Chateau, and Dresden Rose. In the 1930s it used a special mark, "Dresdner Art Germany." Schumann uses high-quality transfer decoration and lovely gilding, and many of its plates have reticulated borders. The company has also copied Helena Wolfsohn's style of courting scenes alternating with flowers. The difference is that Dresden tableware is hand painted, and Schumann is not.

CARL TEICHERT

The Meissen Stove & Porcelain Factory was located in the town of Meissen, Germany, and was begun by Carl Teichert. It operated as such from 1872 to 1945. It was nationalized after World War II. There is much confusion about this company, because its trademark was "MEISSEN" inside an oval with an asterisk at the bottom. It copied the Meissen Blue Onion pattern exactly, hand painting its copies. It made hundreds of dinnerware sets in the Blue Onion pattern.

The company also made decorative porcelain, including some lovely chargers and plates. The quality of the hand paintings on some of the plates produced by this company would rival that of Meissen or Royal Vienna.

Dresden, R. Wehsner, c. 1895 – 1918, artist signed "Vogler." 9½"; hand-painted mythological scene of Venus making love potion, elaborately beaded, jeweled and heavy gold paste border. $800.00 – 900.00. (See mark #32.)

Close-up of border.

Close-up.

Dresden, R. Klemm, c. 1890 – 1916, artist signed "Wagner." 9½"; portrait of beautiful woman with flowing long hair with a rose, exquisite border with turquoise jewels and raised gold paste. $1,000.00 – 1,200.00. (See mark #33.)

Dresden, R. Klemm, c. 1900 – 1920, artist signed "Hautman." 7¾"; marked "Ruschout und Tockter" on back, portrait of lady with her daughter at her side making garland of flowers, heavy gold paste border with beading on green ground, scratch on blue gown. $300.00 – 400.00. (See mark #34.)

Dresden, F. Hirsch, c. 1901 – 1930. 9½"; entitled Mosel, portrait of lovely lady, exceptionally decorated border with medallions of heavy gilt musical instruments, artist palettes, and wine ewers; Tiffany luster. $1,000.00 – 1,200.00.

Close-up of portrait.

Close-up of border.

Close-up.

Close-up of border.

Dresden, A. Lamm, c. 1891 – 1914, S. Lieb. 10¹/₈"; rich cobalt border with elaborate raised paste gilding; portrait of woman leaning on a wall with an Egyptian motif, mountains and town in background, entitled Attentive Nach, D. Coomans. $1,300.00 – 1,500.00. (See mark #35.)

Dresden, A. Lamm, c. 1891 – 1914, artist signed "S. Lieb." 10¹/₈"; rich cobalt border with elaborate raised paste gilding, self-portrait of a happy Rembrandt raising a glass of whisky and holding a lovely lady in his lap, entitled Rembrandt nict Frau. Selbstporträt, a few wear spots. $800.00 – 1,000.00.

Close-up.

Close-up.

Dresden, A. Lamm, c. 1891 – 1914. 9$^{1}/_{2}$"; rich cobalt border with elaborate raised paste gilding, portrait of lady buying a rug from gypsy and his son, entitled Die Wahrsagerin. $900.00 – 1,000.00.

Dresden, A. Lamm, c. 1891 – 1914, artist signed "S. Lieb." 10$^{1}/_{8}$"; rich cobalt border with elaborate raised paste gilding, young girl has blouse caught on a branch and her lover is freeing her. The P. Thumann picture is entitled Uelerraschimg. $1,200.00 – 1,400.00.

Close-up.

Dresden, A. Lamm, c. 1891 – 1914. 9¹/₂"; rich cobalt border with elaborate raised paste gilding, little boy telling his friend a secret. $1,200.00 – 1,400.00.

Close-up.

Dresden, A. Lamm, c. 1891 – 1914, artist signed "S. Lieb." 10¹/₈"; portrait of lady taking an apple from a cherub, entitled Eva Nach E. Bisson, rich cobalt border with elaborate raised paste gilding. $1,200.00 – 1,400.00.

Dresden, A. Lamm, c. 1891 – 1914, artist signed "S. Lieb." 10¹/₈"; entitled Der Erste Kuss (G. Schroedler), rich cobalt border with elaborate raised paste gilding, one rub at bottom left. $800.00 – 900.00.

Dresden, A. Lamm, c. 1891 – 1914, artist signed "O. Dietrich." 10"; rich cobalt border with elaborate raised paste gilding, portrait of girl playing lute. $1,050.00 – 1,150.00.

Dresden, F. Hirsch, c. 1910 – 1920, for Ovington Bros., NY. Scalloped, 8½"; decorated with hand-painted flowers alternating with gilt flowers, borders have network of intricate gold, heavy paste snowflake in center. $75.00 – 100.00. (See mark #36.)

Dresden, Carl Thieme, c. 1920s, for Ovington Bros., NY. Reticulated, 9"; center has hand-painted flowers, the Marie Antoinette monogram, and heavy gold paste decoration. $200.00 – 300.00.

Dresden, R. Klemm, c. 1886 – 1900, artist signed "A. Bock." 9¼"; portrait of woman with flowing hair, entitled Stilles G. Luck, green Tiffany luster border with raised gold paste. $1,000.00 – 1,200.00.

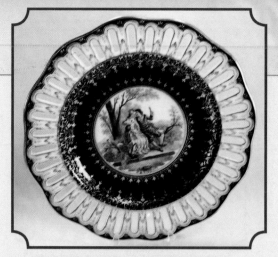

Dresden, R. Klemm, c. 1900. Reticulated, 9¼"; cobalt and gilt border, hand-painted courting scene. $300.00 – 350.00.

Dresden, Donath & Co., Limoges blank, c. 1900 – 1915, distributed by A. Schmidt & Co., NY. Service plate, 10½"; hand-painted flowers and heavy gold paste wreaths and roses. $100.00 – 125.00.

Dresden, Carl Thieme, c. 1920s, made for Ovingtons & Co. Reticulated, 9"; array of hand-painted flowers. $200.00 – 225.00. (See mark #37.)

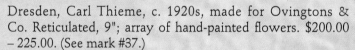

Dresden, R. Klemm, c. 1890 – 1902, artist signed "N. Kaufmann." 4¾"; entitled Abelard und Hyman, apple green border with raised gold paste flower garlands. $200.00 – 250.00.

Dresden, R. Klemm, c. 1900. 9⅓"; inset with two ladies in a garden, four medallions with cupids framed by gold leaves on border, one wear spot on hair of one of the cupids. $500.00 – 600.00.

Dresden, Heufel & Co., c. 1900 – 1920. 9¼"; portrait of woman in a dark red velvet gown with ruffled collar and feathered hat, 2" cobalt blue and gilt border. $500.00 – 600.00. (See mark #38.)

Dresden, A. Hamann, c. 1920 – 1930s. 10"; array of hand-painted flowers, gold band on rim. $75.00 – 100.00.

Dresden, F. Hirsch, c. 1901 – 1930. Service plate, 10¾"; hand-painted courting scenes alternating with flowers on a yellow ground, gilt decoration. $125.00 – 150.00.

Close-up.

Dresden, A. Lamm, Meissen blank, c. 1890 – 1900. 9³/₄"; hand-painted pub scene, gilt border. $600.00 – 700.00. (See mark #39.)

Dresden, H. Wolfsohn, c. 1890s, signed "Wagner." 9³/₄"; portrait of Countess Anna Potocka, burgundy Tiffany luster border with raised gold paste flowers and leaves. $700.00 – 800.00. (See mark #40.)

Dresden, unidentified decorator, c. 1920s, distributed by A. Schmidt & Sons, NY. Scalloped, 9"; vivid hand-painted flowers, gold border. $50.00 – 75.00. (See mark #41.)

Dresden, A. Lamm, c. 1900. Service plate, 10¾"; finely decorated border with heavy gold paste urns and scrolls, hand-painted flowers. $75.00 – 100.00.

Dresden, A. Lamm, c. 1890s. 10"; hand-painted portrait of Mrs. Spencer on border, decorated with heavy gold paste and beads. $200.00 – 250.00.

Close-up.

Close-up.

Dresden, A. Lamm, c. 1890s. 10"; hand-painted portrait of Princess de Lamballe on border, decorated with heavy gold paste and beads. $200.00 – 250.00.

Dresden, R. Klemm, c. 1890s, artist signed "N. Kiesel." 10"; hand-painted portrait of lady with flowers in her hair, magnificent jeweled and beaded border. $1,500.00 – 1,800.00.

Dresden, G. Meyer, c. 1906. 8"; hand-painted floral garland and six floral cartouches with gilt cross-hatching on border, monogram in center. $75.00 – 100.00. (See mark #42.)

Dresden, G. Meyer, c. 1906. 9¼"; cartouche with hand-painted portrait of young woman, gilt monogram in center. $175.00 – 225.00.

Close-up.

Close-up.

Dresden, A. Lamm, c. 1890, artist signed "Danner." 9¹/₂"; garden scene with lady making necklace of daisies, a Cupid shaping arrows and another looking on, framed with heavy gold, aqua border with gilt. $500.00 – 600.00.

Dresden, A. Lamm, c. 1890, artist signed "Danner." 9¹/₂"; garden scene with lady sitting on bench whispering a secret to a Cupid, framed with heavy gold, aqua border with gilt. $500.00 – 600.00.

Close-up.

Dresden, R. Wehsner, c. 1895 – 1918. Cake plate, 7²/₃"; gold ground with turquoise jewels, border of hand-painted flowers. $100.00 – 150.00.

Close-up.

Dresden, R. Klemm, c. 1890s. 9¹/₂"; portrait of Marie Antoinette, ornate border. $1,400.00 – 1,600.00.

Dresden, A. Lamm, c. 1880s, KPM blank. 9¹/₄"; entitled Erwartung, portrait of lady leaning against stone pillars, green border with raised gold roses. $500.00 – 550.00. (See mark #43.)

Dresden, A. Lamm, c. 1880s, KPM blank. 9¼"; entitled Fruhlings Glaube, portrait of lady in white, green border with raised gold roses. $500.00 – 550.00.

Close-up.

Close-up.

Dresden, Alice Hurford, KPM blank, c. 1891. 10¼"; hand-painted courting scene. $300.00 – 400.00.

Dresden, R. Klemm, c. 1900 – 1910. 4³/₄"; entitled Du Schelm, portrait of woman flirting with Cupid, deep maroon border with raised gilt. $200.00 – 250.00.

Dresden, A. Lamm, c. 1895 – 1920. 10"; hand-painted flowers in center, cream border with raised gold decoration. $200.00 – 250.00.

Close-up.

Rare set of 12 game plates. A. Lamm, c. 1890 – 1920. Swirled, 9¹/₈"; hand-painted game birds in natural setting; birds, bugs, and butterflies on borders with gilt. $2,000.00 – 2,500.00.

Dresden, A. Lamm, c. 1890 – 1920. Swirled game plate, 9¹/₈";
hand-painted game birds in natural setting; birds, bugs, and
butterflies on border with gilt. $200.00 – 250.00.

Close-up.

Close-up.

Dresden, A. Lamm, c. 1890 – 1920. Swirled game
plate, 9¹/₈"; hand-painted game birds in natural setting; birds, bugs, and butterflies on border with gilt.
$200.00 – 250.00.

Dresden, A. Lamm, c. 1890 – 1920. Swirled game plate, 9¹⁄₈";
hand-painted game birds in natural setting; birds, bugs, and
butterflies on border with gilt. $200.00 – 250.00.

Close-up.

Dresden, A. Lamm, c. 1890 – 1920. Swirled game plate, 9¹⁄₈"; hand-
painted game birds in natural setting; birds, bugs, and butterflies on border with gilt. $200.00 – 250.00.

Dresden, C. Thieme, c. 1920s. 9¹⁄₂"; well-painted courting scenes
cartouche in center, lavish gold border with floral cartouches and
gold paste leaves and flowers, turquoise jewels. $500.00 – 600.00.

Close-up.

Close-up.

Dresden, C. Thieme, c. 1920s. 9½"; well-painted courting scenes cartouche in center, lavish gold border with floral cartouches and gold paste leaves and flowers, turquoise jewels. $500.00 – 600.00.

Dresden, Donath, c. 1900. 8¾"; aqua Tiffany luster with heavy gold scalloped and cut-out border; center medallion of hand-painted portrait lady holding a rose and with a veil or scarf on her head. $400.00 – 450.00.

Close-up.

Close-up.

Dresden, Heufel & Co., c. 1900 – 1940. 8²/₃" with reticulated border; three charming hand-painted cherubs in center. $300.00 – 350.00.

Dresden, Richard Klemm, c. 1890s. 8³/₄" with reticulated gilt border; center cartouche portraying lovely lady framed by raised gold roses, unusual pale aqua luster ground with gilt floral sprays. $500.00 – 600.00.

Dresden, A. Lamm, c. 1886 – 1890s. 8³/₄"; lovely lady with two Cupids in center, entitled Ver Schossene Pfeile (Shooting Arrows), intricate cobalt blue border with six cartouches of hand-painted flowers. $500.00 – 600.00.

Dresden, A. Lamm, c. 1886 – 1890s. 8³⁄₄"; lovely lady with Cupid and dove in center, entitled Liebersorahel (Oracle of Love), intricate cobalt blue border with six cartouches of hand-painted flowers. $500.00 – 600.00.

Dresden, F. Hirsch, c. 1903 – 1920. Egg server with six receptacles, 10"; hand-painted flowers and gilt. $350.00 – 400.00.

Dresden, R. Klemm, c. 1900 – 1910. 9¹⁄₃"; allegorical scene, ornate border. $500.00 – 600.00.

Dresden, Helena Wolfsohn, c. 1890s. Reticulated, 10¹⁄₄"; hand-painted scene of man and woman on horseback, yellow medallions. $300.00 – 350.00.

Dresden, R. Klemm, c. 1900 – 1920. 8¼"; hand-painted flowers on blue alternating with courting scenes on white, gilt decoration on rim. $75.00 – 100.00.

Dresden, Heufel & Co., c. 1890s. Oyster plate, 8"; six receptacles and one for sauce in center, hand-painted flowers and gilt. $400.00 – 500.00.

Dresden, R. Klemm, c. 1890s. Square-shaped oyster plate, 7⅔"; sandy beige ground with six graduated slightly ribbed wells with two small wells for sauce, hand-painted flowers and gilt. $400.00 – 500.00.

Dresden, R. Wehsner, c. 1890s. 9²/₃"; portrait of Beatrice Cenci after Rini (1577 – 1599), exceptional gilt border. $900.00 – 1,000.00. (See mark #44.)

Close-up.

Close-up.

Dresden, Ambrosius Lamm, c. 1890 – 1914, signed "Schneider." 10"; well-painted portrait of Amalie Kaiserin, cobalt border with heavy gold paste work. $1,200.00 – 1,500.00.

Close-up.

Dresden, Ambrosius Lamm, c. 1890s. Charger, 14"; hand-painted scene of Napoleon on a stallion crossing the Alps, cream border with lavish raised gold. $2,000.00 – 2,500.00.

Close-up.

Close-up of border.

ES Germany (Erdmann Schlegelmilch), c. 1938. Cake plate, 10"; pink and white rose transfer, gilt border. $125.00 – 150.00.

Service Heinrich & Co., c. 1911 – 1934, made for John Wanamaker. Plate, 10³/₄"; two etched gold bands, floral border. $75.00 – 100.00. (See mark #47.)

Hutschenreuther, c. 1950s. Service plate, 10¹/₂"; cobalt blue and cream border overlaid with gilt, center medallion of flower transfer. $100.00 – 125.00. (See mark #48.)

Hutschenreuther, Black Knight, c. 1925 – 1941. 9"; arrangement of roses and orchids in center, cobalt decoration on rim. $75.00 – 85.00. (See mark #49.)

Hutschenreuther, Dresden Studio, c. 1920s, artist signed "Friedrich." 9⁷/₈"; portrait of Ann Hillmayr, cobalt border with gold paste. $1,000.00 – 1,200.00. (See mark #50.)

Hutschenreuther, Dresden Studio, c. 1920s, artist signed "Friedrich." 9⁷/₈"; portrait of Ludwig von Beethoven, cobalt border with gold paste. $1,000.00 – 1,200.00.

Dresden, Hutschenreuther Decorating Studio, c. 1918 – 1945. Service plate, 10³/₄"; border of hand-painted courting scenes alternating with flowers on gold, array of flowers in center. $200.00 – 250.00.

Dresden, Hutschenreuther Decorating Studio, c. 1918 – 1945. 6³/₄"; well-painted portrait of Anna Kaula in center, originally painted by Joseph Stieler in 1829, raised gilt decoration on border. $500.00 – 550.00. (See mark #51.)

Close-up.

KPM, Berlin, c. 1890 – 1920. 8²/₃"; factory-decorated fruit in center, heavy applied gold paste decoration on border. $400.00 – 450.00. (See mark #53.)

KPM, c. 1890 – 1920. 8²/₃"; factory-decorated fruit in center, heavy applied gold paste decoration on border. $400.00 – 450.00.

KPM, c. 1890 – 1920. 8²/₃"; factory-decorated fruit in center, heavy applied gold paste decoration on border. $400.00 – 450.00.

KPM, c. 1837 – 1844. 7"; gold border, hand-painted flowers in center. $200.00 – 250.00. (See mark #54.)

KPM, c. 1890 – 1900. 8³/4", reticulated border; decorated outside the factory, portrait of Queen Louise. (See mark #55.) $850.00 – 950.00.

Close-up.

KPM, c. 1900. 9³/4"; painted outside the factory, Greek Key border, center portrait of lovely Grecian woman looking out to sea. $900.00 – 1,000.00.

Close-up.

Close-up.

KPM, c. 1890s. 9¹/₃"; painted outside the factory, winter scene, light blue and white border with gold ribbons. $350.00 – 450.00. (See mark #56.)

Close-up.

KPM, c. 1880s. 8³/₄", reticulated border with gilt scrolls; factory decorated, beautiful array of pomegranates, purple plums, and flowers. $500.00 – 600.00.

KPM, c. 1900. 8¹⁄₄"; factory-decorated hand-painted apples and apple blossoms, rich cobalt blue border with heavy raised gold decoration. $500.00 – 600.00.

Close-up of border.

KPM, c. 1900. 8¹⁄₄"; factory-decorated hand-painted fruit, rich cobalt blue border with heavy raised gold decoration. $500.00 – 600.00.

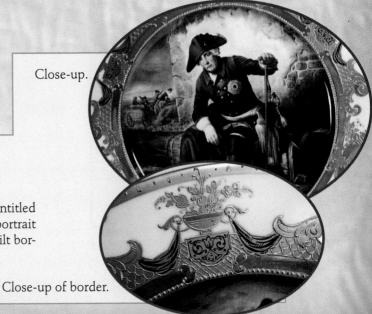

Close-up.

KPM, painted outside factory, c. 1870. 10¹⁄₃"; entitled Friedrich der Grosse Nach Hallin, hand-painted portrait of King Frederick in his military uniform, lavish gilt border. $1,200.00 – 1,300.00.

Close-up of border.

KPM, painted outside factory by Dresden decorator Grace H. Bishop, c. 1890s. 8"; adorable portrait of Zuleika, cobalt border with pearl jeweling, gold beads and gilt flowers and leaves. $800.00 – 1,000.00. (See mark #57.)

Close-up.

KPM, Berlin, c. 1900 – 1920. 8²/₃", with reticulated border; Purple Indian design with Oriental flowers and bugs. $275.00 – 300.00. (See mark #58.)

KPM Berlin, c. 1920s. 8¹/₂"; hand-painted flowers, raised gold flowers. $200.00 – 250.00.

KPM, painted outside factory, c. 1890s, artist signed "L. Lang." Charger, 14"; hand-painted scene of lady and her lover dancing in wooded setting. $600.00 – 650.00.

KPM, Berlin, c. 1910. 8¼"; Art Nouveau jeweled design with hand-enameled grapes and cherries, heavy gold paste branches. $300.00 – 350.00.

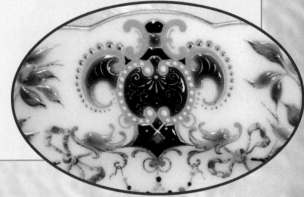

Close-up of jeweled border.

KPM, Berlin, c. 1930 – 1950. Charger, 14"; hand-painted flowers and insects. $500.00 – 550.00. (See mark #59.)

Close-up.

KPM, c. 1837 – 1844. 7"; hand-painted flowers in center, gold border. $200.00 – 250.00. (See mark #60.)

KPM, c. 1837 – 1844. 7"; hand-painted flowers in center, gold border. $200.00 – 250.00.

KPM, c. 1837 – 1844. 7"; hand-painted flowers in center, gold border. $200.00 – 250.00.

KPM, c. 1837 – 1844. 7"; hand-painted flowers in center, gold border. $200.00 – 250.00.

KPM Berlin, c. 1900 – 1920. Reticulated cake plate, 8¹/₃" hand-painted flowers, ornate gilt border. $400.00 – 450.00.

KPM, decorated outside factory, c. 1900. 9¹/₄"; hand-painted flowers, gilt border. $150.00 – 200.00.

KPM Berlin, c. 1900. 8¹/₂"; well-painted flowers, gilt border. $300.00 – 350.00.

KPM Berlin, c. 1900 – 1920. Reticulated, 9¼"; hand-painted apples and blossoms, gilt decoration. $400.00 – 450.00.

Joseph Kuba, Bavaria, c. 1950 – 1980. 10½"; courting scene transfer, blue ground with gold floral border. $40.00 – 60.00.

Meissen, c. 1930 – 1950s. Charger, 11"; hand-painted flowers, floral cartouches framed by heavy gold. $400.00 – 450.00. (See mark #89.)

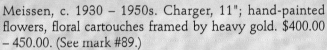

Meissen, c. 1850 – 1900. Charger, 9¼"; magnificent hand-painted allegorical scene. $3,000.00 – 3,500.00.

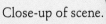

Close-up of scene.

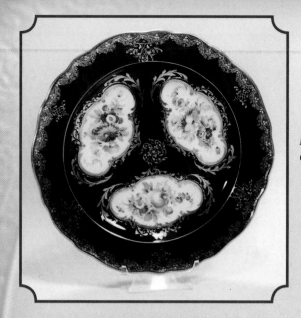

Meissen, c. 1850 – 1924. 9¾"; cobalt blue with hand-painted flowers in white cartouches, gilt. $500.00 – 550.00. (See mark #90.)

Meissen, c. 1850 – 1924. 9¾"; exceptional hand-painted flowers on unusual chocolate brown ground. $1,500.00 – 1,600.00.

Close-up of flower painting.

Meissen, c. 1850 – 1924. Two-handled cake plate, 11½"; hand-painted rose in center, buds on border, no gilt. $150.00 – 200.00.

Meissen, c. 1924 – 1934, two incised marks. Round scalloped serving plate, 11"; roses and gilt. $300.00 – 350.00. (See mark #91.)

Close-up.

Meissen, c. 1924 – 1934. Charger, 11½"; hand-painted fruit in center, heavy gold flowers and leaves around border. $500.00 – 600.00. (See mark #92.)

Close-up of gold flowers.

Close-up of fruit.

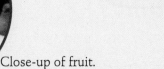

Meissen, c. 1887 – 1924. Scalloped, 6³/4"; Rich Onion pattern, red and blue fruits and flowers with gilt. $100.00 – 150.00.

Meissen, c. 1850 – 1887. Scalloped and ribbed charger, 12"; Blue Onion pattern with gilt rim. $500.00 – 600.00.

Meissen, c. 1888 – 1924. 8¹/2", reticulated border; Blue Onion pattern. $200.00 – 250.00.

Close-up of gilding.

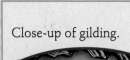

Close-up of center.

Meissen, c. 1924 – 1934. Scalloped charger, 11¹/4"; array of hand-painted flowers in center, border has lavish gold flowers and ornate scrolls. $500.00 – 600.00.

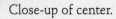

Meissen, c. 1850 – 1900. Scalloped, 9¼"; hand-painted courting scene in center, yellow ground with enamel flowers and gold beads, border has three cartouches with purple monochrome courting scenes. $700.00 – 800.00.

Close-up of courting scene.

Close-up of purple monochrome.

Close-up.

Meissen, c. 1850 – 1900. Charger, 13"; well-painted pastoral scene in center, three cartouches with purple monochrome courting scenes framed by gilt on border. $900.00 – 1,000.00.

Meissen, c. 1850 – 1900. 10"; center cartouche with hand-painted fruit, cobalt border with gilt leaves. $700.00 – 750.00.

Meissen, c. 1950s. Scalloped charger, 11"; hand-painted flowers and floral cartouches on white. $300.00 – 400.00.

Meissen, c. 1830s. 7³/₄"; colorful hand-painted embossed flowers in center, jeweled and gilt border. $200.00 – 300.00. (See mark #93.)

Close-up of center.

Meissen, c. 1850 – 1924. 9½"; heavy gold grapes and leaves around the border, array of hand-painted flowers in center. $400.00 – 500.00.

Meissen, c. 1850 – 1900. Platter, 2" x 9"; two hand-painted swans in relief, a flying crane and one with fish in mouth, ribbed border with gilt trim. $1,800.00 – 2,000.00.

Close-up.

Meissen, c. 1850 – 1924. Charger, 11³/₄"; array of hand-painted fruit, rich cobalt border with white and gold grape leaves. $600.00 – 700.00.

Close-up.

Meissen, c. 1850 – 1924. Charger, 11¾"; array of hand-painted fruit, rich cobalt border with white and gold grape leaves. $600.00 – 700.00.

Meissen, c. 1930 – 1950. Charger, 12"; hand-painted flowers in center, four heavy cobalt cartouches with heavy gilt roses. $700.00 – 800.00.

Close-up of gilt roses.

Close-up.

Meissen, painted outside factory, c. 1915 – 1919. 9"; center hand-painted Cupids, ornate border with gilt urns, forget-me-nots and gold dots. $600.00 – 650.00.

Meissen, c. 1850 – 1924. 10¹/₃"; hand-painted flowers center, outstanding gilding on border. $500.00 – 600.00.

Nymphenburg, c. 1890 – 1895. Reticulated, 8¹/₄"; cobalt petal-shaped cartouche with gilt, three floral reserves. $300.00 – 350.00. (See mark #103.)

Close-up.

Nymphenburg, c. 1862 – 1887. Dessert plate with reticulated border, 8"; hand-painted fruit and flower blossoms in center, cobalt and gilt border. $400.00 – 450.00.

Otto Reinecke, Maschendorf Porcelain Manufactory, c. 1900 – 1945. Platter, 15" x 10"; Phoenix Bird Motif. $125.00 – 145.00.

Rosenthal, c. 1939 – 1945. Octagonal, 8³⁄₄"; dark red border, gilt decoration, floral transfer in center. $50.00 – 75.00. (See mark #128.)

Rosenthal, c. 1939 – 1945. Scalloped, 9¹⁄₄"; dark red border, gilt decoration, floral transfer in center. $75.00 – 100.00.

Rosenthal, c. 1945 – 1949, marked "Continental Ivory." Service plate, 10³⁄₄"; vivid flowers and gilt on an ivory ground. $75.00 – 100.00. (See mark #129.)

Rosenthal, c. 1949 – 1950. Service plate, 10³/₄"; floral transfer in center surrounded by gilt decoration, cobalt border with gilt scrolls. $100.00 – 125.00.

Close-up of center medallion.

The same, set of 12. $1,000.00 – 1,500.00.

Rosenthal, c. 1891 – 1904. 8³/₄"; gold border with underglaze blue floral transfer decoration. $50.00 – 75.00. (See mark #130.)

Rosenthal, c. 1898 – 1906. Scalloped, 8½"; transfer flowers in center, cobalt blue border with gilt flowers. $75.00 – 100.00. (See mark #131.)

The same, set of 12. $800.00 – 1,200.00.

Royal Bayreuth (Sontag & Sons), c. 1887 – 1902. Swirled, 9"; Oriental underglaze blue floral pattern. $75.00 – 100.00.

Royal Bayreuth (Sontag & Sons), c. 1887 – 1902. Scalloped, 8½"; Oriental underglaze blue floral pattern. $75.00 – 100.00. (See mark #132.)

Royal Bonn (F. A. Mehlem), c. 1890 – 1920. Earthenware, 7¾"; blue and white floral transfer. $50.00 – 75.00.

RS Prussia, c. 1904. Scalloped cake plate with crimped edges, 9¾", two handles; lovely floral transfer. $250.00 – 300.00.

Close-up.

Schumann, Carl, c. 1930s. Service plate, 10¾"; array of floral transfers in center, floral cartouches on border overlaid with gold. $75.00 – 100.00. (See mark #136.)

Schumann, Carl, c. 1918. Scalloped service plate, 11"; unusual white roses with gold on black, gilt scrolling, cream ground. $75.00 – 100.00. (See mark #137.)

Schumann, Carl, US Zone, c. 1945 – 1949. 9¼"; floral transfer, reticulated border. $90.00 – 115.00. (See mark #138.)

Schumann, F. A. (Friedrich Adolph), Berlin, c. 1835 – 1869, artist signed "Schonfeldt Eisner." 9½"; hand-painted portrait of Napoleon with coat of arms, cobalt border with etched gold rim. $600.00 – 750.00. (See mark #139.)

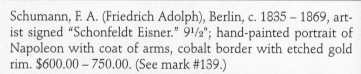

Close-up of portrait.

Close-up of coat-of-arms.

Schumann, F. A. (Friedrich Adolph), Berlin, c. 1835 – 1869, artist signed "Schonfeldt Eisner." 9¹/₂"; hand-painted portrait of Josephine, cobalt border with etched gold rim. $600.00 – 750.00.

Schumann, F. A. (Friedrich Adolph), Berlin, c. 1835 – 1869, artist signed "Schonfeldt Eisner." 9¹/₂"; hand-painted portrait of Madame Juliet Recamier, cobalt border with etched gold rim. $600.00 – 750.00.

Close-up.

Close-up.

Teichert, Ernst, Meissen, c. 1884 – 1912, artist signed "K. T. Schapek." Earthenware charger, 11"; hand-painted gypsy with flowing black hair. $500.00 – 600.00. (See mark #144.)

Teichert, Ernst, Meissen, c. 1882 – 1930. Charger, 11⅓"; portrait of a young girl with Alps in background, cobalt border elaborate raised gold. $1,000.00 – 1,200.00. (See mark #145.)

Tirschenreuth Porcelain Factory, c. 1960 – 1970s. Service plate, 11"; center medallion of flowers, hand decorated gold on cream. $60.00 – 95.00. (See mark #146.)

Volkstedt, Richard Eckert Factory, c. 1894 – 1918, artist signed "A. Berker." 10"; portrait of three children looking into a bucket, cobalt luster border with heavy hand-gilt paste. $1,100.00 – 1,200.00. (See mark #156.)

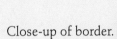

Close-up.

Close-up of border.

Unidentified mark, E. R. P. & Co., Germany, distributed by Paul's Gifts, c. 1945 – 1949 (U.S. Zone). Octagonal plate with reticulation, 8½"; courting scene transfer in center. $40.00 – 60.00.

Unmarked, probably Bavarian, c. 1900. Scalloped cake plate with two handles, 10³/₈"; figural transfer in center, cobalt border with gilt flowers. $75.00 – 100.00.

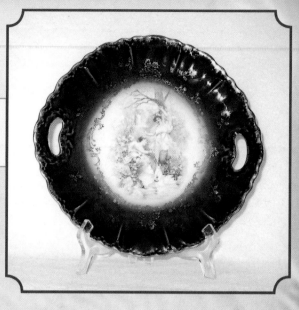

Unknown maker, c. 1900, artist signed "A. Delade." Charger, 12"; hand-painted mums. $100.00 – 150.00.

Unmarked, probably German, c. 1930s. Charger, 12"; hand-painted view of Albrechtsburg in Meissen. $100.00 – 150.00.

Unmarked, probably German, c. 1890s. 7½"; hand-painted portrait of young girl in native Austrian costume on gold, rubbing on gold. $150.00 – 200.00.

Close-up.

Unmarked, probably German, c. 1880s. Oyster plate with five oyster-shaped wells, ribbing on edge; white with pink shading in wells, gilt trim. $100.00 – 125.00.

Dresden style, marked "R. B." 8", reticulated border; mixed floral decoration. $50.00 – 60.00.

Dresden style, unmarked. Scalloped, 9¼"; hand-painted portrait of baby, dark red Tiffany, or luster, glaze, raised gold paste. $700.00 – 900.00.

Close-up.

Bawo & Dotter, Austria, made for Higgins and Setzer, c. 1884 – 1914. 9"; excellent quality floral transfer. $40.00 – 50.00. (See mark #3.)

Bawo & Dotter, Austria, made for Higgins and Setzer, c. 1884 – 1914. 9"; excellent quality floral transfer. $40.00 – 50.00.

OTHER EUROPEAN PLATES

 AUSTRIA

ROYAL VIENNA

The Vienna Porcelain Factory was founded by Claudius du Paquier in 1717. It was second to Meissen in producing hard-paste porcelain. The company began producing cabinet ware derived from silver shapes and decorated with Chinese motifs and exotic flowers.

Financial difficulties forced du Paquier to sell his factory to the state in 1744. At that time the Vienna mark, a shield incised or in underglaze blue, was first introduced. It represented the banded shield from the center of the Austrian royal coat of arms (*bindenschild*). Viewed upside down, it gave the impression of a beehive mark.

From 1747 to 1784 the company reached its peak of fame. The chief modeler, Johann Niedermeyer, introduced new background colors. A fine cobalt blue rivaled the Sevres bleu roi. Today this cobalt blue shade is still a favorite with collectors. Exquisite cabinet ware with portrait and landscape medallions on colored grounds with gold decoration was produced for members of royalty and their families. Richly ornamental cabinet ware was made in the neoclassical and Empire styles, often decorated with magnificent reproductions of paintings by famous artists as well as beautiful floral and elaborate gilding.

During the period between 1784 and 1830, the decoration of Vienna cabinet plates was among the finest in Europe. Plates had colored grounds with lavish gilding and rich painting. Very little of the white body of the porcelain was left showing. Classical subjects, landscapes, and topographical views were in the centers of plates or on reserved panels. In the 1820s, botanical plates with accurate depictions of plants charmed the Viennese court.

In 1864 the imperial factory closed because of industrialization and rapidly growing competition. Royal Vienna's stock was sold off to the factory's best painters and gilders, who, finding themselves out of work, set up their own decorating studios and workshops.

ROYAL VIENNA STYLE — THE BEST

Royal Vienna became a style in the late nineteenth century. Porcelain-decorating studios in Berlin, Vienna, and Dresden copied the early Vienna style and produced some exceptional cabinet ware. Many of the blanks already had the imperial shield mark. The decorators produced cabinet plates that closely approached the style and quality of those of the Vienna factory. Other studios copied the Vienna shield mark in the hopes it would enhance their wares. Today it remains the most copied mark of all time.

The better-quality Royal Vienna–style plates had center subjects or portraits and ornate borders with raised gilt. Borders were often cobalt blue, dark red, or emerald green. Today these plates can be found with a variety of hand-painted subjects. Plates with allegorical scenes were usually copied from oil paintings displayed in the European museums. Those that bring the highest prices are the plates with children and beautiful women. The most popular women's portraits found on the Royal Vienna–style plates are those of Cleopatra, Queen Louise, Ann Hillmayr, and French court beauties Marie Antoinette, Josephine, Princess Lambelle, Countess Potacka, and Madame Recamier.

One of the best studios decorating in the Vienna style was that of Ernst Wahliss. In 1902 Wahliss, who owned a porcelain company in Turn-Teplitz, Bohemia, bought a considerable number of molds from the Imperial Royal Factory. He opened a studio in Vienna and began making reproductions. Wahliss produced high-quality cabinet plates.

Joseph Ahne had a porcelain and glass decorating studio in Steinschonau, Bohemia, around 1894. He painted Royal Vienna–style plates of famous people, such as President William McKinley. His portraits had outstanding lifelike detail. They were so realistic they almost looked like photographs.

Franz Xaver Thallmaier had a porcelain-decorating studio in Munich. His specialty was portraits, and he produced some outstanding Royal Vienna–style plates between around 1888 and 1907. He selected female portraits after the artist Joseph Stieler. Most of his plates had a plain cobalt border, which suggests that he did not employ a skilled gilder in his shop.

ROYAL VIENNA STYLE — THE WORST

Around the turn of the twentieth century, hundreds of companies in Germany, Austria, and Bohemia copied the bindenschild mark and produced plates with transfers of mythological scenes or portraits. The most popular transfers were taken from Angelica Kauffman's paintings. (Angelica Kauffman, 1741 – 1807, was a Swiss painter who painted many mythological and historical scenes.) These sets are often of mediocre or poor quality and should not be confused with hand-painted sets with rich background work.

CONFUSION OVER MARK

Most of the portrait and allegorical plates that come on the market today are not true Royal Vienna, as they

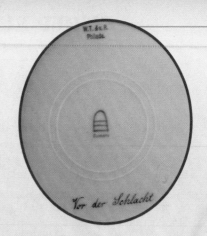

were produced after 1864. Dealers and collectors alike mistakenly believe that if a shield mark is under the glaze, it is a true Vienna mark. There are 40 or more correct Royal Vienna marks. It takes an expert to detect the subtle differences. There are several indicators to tell for sure if it is a fake:

1. If "Royal Vienna" or any title or description is somewhere on the mark.

2. If the mark is blue overglaze. (A blue underglaze mark doesn't necessarily make it authentic either.)

3. Stamped blue underglaze

4. If letters or inscriptions are arranged to make the mark appear as a beehive.

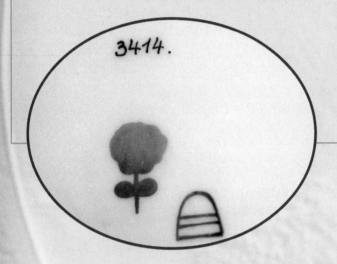

❀ CZECHOSLOVAKIA ❀

CHARLES AHRENFELDT

Charles Ahrenfeldt had a porcelain manufactory in Limoges, France, and a decorating shop in Altrohlau, Bohemia (now Stara Role, Czech Republic), from 1886 to 1910. He decorated unmarked porcelain blanks from local factories near Karlsbad and applied his own marks. The company also imported porcelain from the von Schierholz Company in Plaue, Germany. Ahrenfeldt decorated hand-painted reticulated plates and tea wares in the Dresden style.

PIRKENHAMMER

In 1803, Frederic Höcke founded the Pirkenhammer Company in Pirkenhammer, Bohemia, which is presently Brezova in the Czech Republic. The company produced household porcelain and had many owners. Fischer & Mieg brought it to prominence from around 1857 to 1918. Many lovely tableware and decorative cabinet plates with hand-painted flowers and gilt were made during this period.

DENMARK

BING & GRØNDAHL

Brothers Meyer and Jacob Bing owned a shop in Copenhagen that sold books, stationery, and art objects. When the famous sculptor Frederick Veilhelm Grøndahl joined them, the three organized the Bing & Grøndahl Porcelain Factory in 1853. About a year and a half later young Grøndahl died, and craftsmen were bought in from abroad. Little by little the company flourished.

Harold Bing, Artistic Director of Bing & Grøndahl, who conceived idea of celebrating Christmas with a special plate, 1906 (courtesy of Royal Copenhagen, Frederiksberg, Denmark).

The Bing & Grøndahl Factory, c. 1860 (courtesy of Royal Copenhagen, Frederiksberg, Denmark).

At first the manufactory sold figurines, and as it became more successful, it branched out into dinnerware and coffee services. Its trademark is taken from the Three

was appointed to the Royal Courts of Denmark, Sweden, and Great Britain.

In 1895, F. A. Hallin designed the first limited-edition plate to commemorate the holiday season. Hallin believed that a northern landscape in the snow, with a dark sky and shades of bluish white, would be well suited for the limited palette of underglaze painting. The plate, entitled "Beyond the Frozen Window," pictured Copenhagen's picturesque skyline as seen through a frosted windowpane. About 500 were produced, and each sold for 50 cents. When Harold Bing ordered his potters to destroy the mold for the plate, thus establishing the first known limited-edition collector's plate, little did anyone realize a new custom was being established. Only 13 of these plates are known to still exist. Today, F. A. Hallin's design is sought after by collectors and sells for up to $8,000.00 in the secondary market.

The painting ladies at Bing & Grøndahl (courtesy of Royal Copenhagen, Frederiksberg, Denmark).

Towers in the coat-of-arms of the city of Denmark. The Bing & Grøndahl Company received high honors and

The first Christmas plate, Bing & Grøndahl, c. 1895, "Behind the Frozen Window" by F. A. Hallin (courtesy of Royal Copenhagen, Frederiksberg, Denmark).

ROYAL COPENHAGEN

The Royal Copenhagen Porcelain Manufactory was established in Copenhagen in 1779. It was financially supported by the royal family; Queen Juliane Marie took special interest in its production. It was her idea to have three blue wavy lines, symbolizing the three Danish waterways, as the company's trademark. In 1868 Royal Copenhagen ceased being state owned, and in 1884 the factory was moved from the city of Copenhagen to the rural suburb of Frederiksberg.

In 1790 the company produced one of the most prestigious and oldest dinner services in production today, Flora Danica. The eighteenth century was the Age of Enlightenment, and many new natural sciences, such as botany, were developed. In 1761 George Christian Oeder, director of the new botanical gardens in Copenhagen, decided to publish an encyclopedia of the national flora of Denmark. The publication was called *Flora Danica*, and it took over 100 years to complete. It included 3,000 hand-colored copperplate prints depicting every wild plant of the nation, including mosses, fungi, ferns, and flowers.

Crown Prince Frederick, later King Frederick VI, was pleased with the progress of this new folio and decided to commission a dinner service from Royal Copenhagen and decorated with flora from the new publication. He needed a gift for Czarina Catherine II of Russia and thought a beautiful dinner set depicting the nation's flora would be a worthy gift for a member of royalty.

The monumental task of transferring the flora from the folio on to a dinner service was given to Johann Christoph Boyer, one of the most talented and sensitive artists of the late eighteenth century. The Flora Danica dinner service was to be Boyer's lifework. It ultimately deprived him of all his strength and destroyed his eyesight, as he had to work in poor light during the long dark winter months in Denmark. He did almost all the hand-painted floral decoration on the 1,802 individual pieces himself. Finally the project came to an end in 1802 when Boyer could no longer work. By this time Catherine had died, and it was decided that the Flora Danica service would remain in Denmark as the heritage of the Danish kings.

Flora Danica is still being made today. It takes considerable artistic skill to paint the flora and takes more than 12,000 individual brush strokes to complete one

dinner plate. Prices are high for Flora Danica pieces, and the market is brisk. Dinner plates retail from $700.00 to $900.00.

Royal Copenhagen's most well-known pattern, Blue Fluted, is of Chinese origin and was created in 1780. It has three edge forms: smooth edge, closed-lace edge, and perforated-lace edge. It is still very popular today and is called the national tableware of Denmark. Another famous pattern, Blue Flower, was first designed in 1775. The blue bouquets are still painted by hand and include roses, tulips, poppies, and carnations. Each piece carries the signature of the painter. There are three different versions of Blue Flower: angular, curved, and braided.

Royal Copenhagen is world renowned for its outstanding examples of underglaze painting, developed by Arnold Krog (1856 – 1931). An architect by training, he was invited by the director of the factory to create something innovative in the field of porcelain. During the winter of 1884/1885, inspiration came to Krog. Looking at an old blue plate, he was fascinated by its beauty. He thought that if it were possible to paint blue dots and lines underglaze, it should surely be possible to paint other things as well. He visualized how an opaque glaze could bring out the radiant beauty of the Danish winter landscape better than any other technique.

Krog was appointed art director, and he immediately surrounded himself with new talent. He encouraged his artists to experiment with underglaze painting. One of his assistants was the painter F. A. Hallin, who produced outstanding work in this new technique. Hallin and Krog won awards at the great Scandinavian Exhibition at Copenhagen in 1888 and at the Paris Exhibition. The new Royal Copenhagen products were awarded the Grand Prix d'Honneur — a unique distinction. In 1895, Hallin left to work for the Bing & Grøndahl Factory.

In 1908 Royal Copenhagen followed Bing & Grøndahl's example by producing its own series of Christmas plates. Its first plate was the "Madonna and Child" by C. Thomsen and sold for $1.00. Today it is worth $3,000.00 – 4,000.00 on the secondary market.

Today the Royal Copenhagen and Bing & Grøndahl companies, as well as Georg Jensen and Holmegaard Glassworks, are united under one name — Royal Copenhagen. Each company has retained its own unique qualities.

HUNGARY

Herend Porcelain was founded in 1826 by V. Stengl. Around 1839, Mór Fischer bought the company and led it to fame with his reproductions of Chinese porcelain. At the Great Exhibition in 1851 at the Crystal Palace in London, the beautiful dinner, tea, and coffee services exhibited by Fischer were admired by all and brought worldwide recognition to the Herend company.

Early Herend tableware was influenced by Meissen decoration, with basket-weave and pierced borders and the typical floral bouquet as a central motif. Most Herend porcelain is painted by hand by talented porcelain painters. Throughout the years, Herend's philosophy has been to keep old traditions while honoring the spirit of the times.

One of the most popular Herend patterns is Rothschild Birds — a series of 12 different multicolored birds depicted in a variety of ways, such as singing, perched in a tree, or in pairs surrounded by tiny insects. The ornate Chinese Bouquet pattern, found in green, blue, rust, and pink, is also a collector favorite.

Another famous pattern was produced in 1851 for the London World Exhibition in 1851. Queen Victoria liked it so much, she commissioned a large table service for Windsor Castle. The pattern became known as Queen Victoria and remains one of Herend's most popular patterns today.

Herend is the largest maker of hand-decorated porcelain in the world today. It employs 1,560 people, including 700 painters and 35 master painters. According to Herend, no other porcelain manufacturer has as many items or patterns in its inventory. Thousands of shapes are available, in more than 5,000 different patterns.

One reason collectors appreciate Herend china is the amount of handwork that goes in each piece of dinnerware. Painters earn the right to sign their names alongside the Herend logo on the base of each piece they decorate. For collectors, such pieces are among Herend's most sought-after items.

ITALY

MAJOLICA

The famous Ginori factory was established in Milan in 1735. It is still in operation today as the Societa Ceramica Italiana Richard Ginori. One of the company's head chemists, Giusto Giusti, began experimenting with traditional majolica techniques in the 1840s, and the company began producing outstanding examples of Victorian majolica in the 1850s. Ginori made monumental display vases and wall plaques to decorate the halls and stairwells of middle-class Victorian homes. Most majolica items made by Ginori are marked with a crown above "GINORI."

Another large producer of nineteenth-century Italian majolica was Ulisse Cantagalli in Florence. From the 1870s until 1901, Ulisse Cantagalli produced a tremendous output of majolica at moderate prices. A company catalog dated 1895 lists almost 1,100 items in majolica. Cantagalli's early wares were replicas of the reliefs by della Robbia. His luster glazes showed a strong Hispano-Moresque influence. Majolica items by Cantagalli are impressed with "CANTAGAL FIRENCE" and an encircled rooster seal.

Majolica is still being made and sold throughout Italy. Tourist souvenirs are one source of the modern Italian majolica found in the marketplace today. Pieces can be found that have incredible shapes and color combinations. A number of twentieth-century Italian majolica pieces are decorated with a technique called *sgraffito*, which is the Italian word for "scratched." The designs are applied by cutting through the slip decoration to the body underneath.

Italian majolica items made from 1900 though the 1950s are often marked with "MADE IN ITALY" painted freehand. More recent pieces have stamped inscriptions or paper labels. Today there is a great new appreciation of new Italian majolica, and much is being made in the town of Orvieto.

CAPODIMONTE STYLE

In the latter part of the nineteenth century, Ginori in Italy and Ernst Bohne in Rudolstadt, Germany, created exquisite dinnerware in the Capodimonte style. The trademark used was a blue or black underglaze crown over an *N*, the old Capodimonte mark. Plates were hand painted with mythological figures, family scenes with landscapes in relief, cavorting cupids, or armorial crests. Grounds are white or all gold with white cloud formations. Some examples of Capodimonte-style plates can be found that were further decorated by Paris painters, usually with a flower painting in the center. These have both a Paris and Crown N mark on the back.

PIERO FORNASETTI

Piero Fornasetti (1913 – 1988) was a painter, sculptor, designer, and decorator from Milan. He created his unique style and worked in almost every medium, including pottery. His sometimes unsettling images were based on nature — the sun, fish, flowers. He collaborated with pottery manufacturers to produce some delightful plates and chargers.

Russian porcelain had a disastrous beginning, but eventually porcelain of fine quality was produced. Peter the Great's daughter, Empress Elizabeth, contracted with a German vagrant, C. K. Hunger, in 1744 to invent porcelain at a factory in St. Petersburg. Unfortunately, Hunger was an adventurer and a con man and constantly made excuses for his failure to make satisfactory porcelain. During three years he barely turned out a dozen items, and they were crooked and discolored.

The Imperial Factory came into its own during the reign of Catherine II, 1762 – 1792. Catherine had a passion for building and for filling what she built with beautiful objects. She personally inspected the factory in 1763 and ordered that highly skilled artisans be hired from Germany, Austria, and France, regardless of the expense.

In 1765, one of the most splendid services was made for Count Grigory Orlov, one of the conspirators who placed Empress Catherine II on the throne. The Count's initials decorated the centers of the plates. The borders were decorated with gold and silver touched with dots of blue enamel.

Catherine's son, the Emperor Paul (1756 – 1801), hated his domineering mother but shared her passion for good porcelain. In 1801 he received a new dinnerware service that he had ordered, one with architectural scenes. He was very pleased with it and pronounced that day to be the happiest in his whole life. As it turned out, it was also the last full day of his life. The following day he was murdered by rival factions.

The art of porcelain making at the Imperial Factory reached its highest point in the first half of the nineteenth century, under Alexander I and Nicholas I. Following Russia's victory over Napoleon in 1812, military themes were popular decorations. A magnificent set of early-nineteenth-century Russian plates were made by the Imperial Factory, painted with military and equestrian scenes with coats of arms. They were framed by delicately tooled gilt borders with trophies and eagles in the Empire style.

The first mark of the Imperial Factory, during the reigns of Elizabeth and Peter III, was a black or impressed double-headed eagle. From the time of Catherine II and through all subsequent rulers, the mark consisted of the reigning sovereign's initials painted under the glaze. These initials were surmounted by the Imperial Crown, except during the reign of Catherine. Imperial porcelain is highly collectible today, and prices are quite high.

After the Revolution, the Imperial Factory became the State Porcelain Works. Later it was renamed Lomonosov, in honor of the founder of the Russian Academy of Science. The most famous dinnerware pattern is Cobalt Net, a dramatic diamond-shaped design in deep cobalt blue and gold. The Lomonosov Porcelain Company is still active today, but many collectors prefer the earlier pieces with the mark "Made in USSR" rather than the current mark, "Made in Russia."

 SWEDEN

The Gefle Porcelain Works was established in 1850. The company produced earthenware from 1850 to 1910, when it changed to porcelain production. It made dinnerware, tea, and coffee services. Famous Swedish painter and designer Arthur Percy was the artistic director from 1923 to 1954. He combined rococo forms with Art Deco patterns. His pattern Flow Blue Vinranka is a deep cobalt blue design of vines, leaves, berries, and flying insects. It is very popular today.

Bawo & Dotter, Austria, made for Higgins and Setzer, c. 1884 – 1914. 9"; excellent quality floral transfer. $40.00 – 50.00.

Bawo & Dotter, Austria, made for Higgins and Setzer, c. 1884 – 1914. 9"; excellent quality floral transfer. $40.00 – 50.00.

MZ Austria (Moritz Zdekauer), c. 1884 – 1909. Scalloped, 8¾"; hand-painted violets, signed "A. B.," probably home decorated. $50.00 – 75.00.

Royal Vienna style, c. 1890s, overglaze shield mark, artist signed "Hauser." 7¼"; portrait of Cupid kissing a lady, pink border with hand-gilt decoration. $300.00 – 350.00. (See mark #148.)

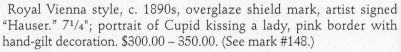

Royal Vienna style, c. 1890s, overglaze shield mark, artist signed "Hauser." 7¼"; portrait of Cupid sharpening his arrow with a lady on a bench, pink border with hand-gilt decoration. $300.00 – 350.00.

Close-up.

Close-up of dog.

Royal Vienna style, underglaze shield mark, c. 1880s, artist signed "H. Firth." 9½"; rare portrait of well-painted collie dog, ornate flowers and scrolls on border. $1,500.00 – 1,700.00.

Royal Vienna style, underglaze shield mark, c. 1880s. 9¹/₂"; intricate border with heavy gold paste decoration, well-painted center portrait of Falstaff holding a jug of wine. $1,200.00 – 1,300.00. (See mark #149.)

Close-up.

Royal Vienna style, underglaze shield mark, c. 1890s. 9¹/₂"; portrait of Rembrandt, unusual cloisonné effect on border. $1,200.00 – 1,300.00. (See mark #150.)

Close-up of border.

Royal Vienna style, underglaze shield mark, c. 1890s, artist signed "Paul Thumann." Plaque, 16½"; portrait of beautiful woman with feathered hat on gold ground, dark red border with intricate gilt decoration. $1,800.00 – 2,000.00.

Royal Vienna style, underglaze shield mark, c. 1890s, artist signed "Paul Thumann." Plaque, 16½"; portrait of beautiful woman with feathered hat on gold ground, dark red border with intricate gilt decoration. $1,800.00 – 2,000.00.

Royal Vienna style, underglaze shield mark, c. 1890s, artist signed "Rock." 9½", marked "Geheimnifs by Wunsch" on back; painting of a little boy telling a secret to his friend, unusual Art Nouveau champlevé enamel–style border with pearl jeweling. $1,200.00 – 1,500.00.

Close-up.

Royal Vienna style, underglaze shield mark, c. 1900. 7³/₄"; hand-painted portrait on gold of little girl with long blonde hair and a bonnet of daisies, dark red border with gold paste flowers. $500.00 – 600.00.

Royal Vienna style, underglaze shield mark, c. 1870s, artist signed "Wagner." 9¹/₂"; well-painted portrait of Cleopatra, cobalt border with heavy gold paste. $1,400.00 – 1,500.00.

Royal Vienna style, overglaze shield mark, c. 1900. 9¹/₈"; hand-painted portrait of lady reading a book in mountain setting, green and red cartouches with gilt decoration and pearl jeweling on border. $500.00 – 600.00. (See mark #151.)

Royal Vienna style, underglaze shield mark, c. 1850 – 1860, signed "A. Berger." Charger or plaque, 14"; outstanding allegorical scene, entitled Achillus als München Verklidt, border with intricate enamels and gilding. $2,700.00 – 3,000.00.

Close-up of border.

Close-up.

Royal Vienna style, overglaze shield mark, c. 1890 – 1920, signed "L. Gurkina." 10½"; portrait of lady with falcon, dark red border with elaborate gilding. $1,200.00 – 1,300.00. (See mark #152.)

Close-up.

Close-up border.

Royal Vienna style, underglaze shield mark, c. 1890s. 9½"; intricate border with raised gilding and beads, portrait of young artist boy in a garden setting and leaning on a Grecian stone pillar with a ram's head. $1,000.00 – 1,200.00.

Close-up.

Royal Vienna style, underglaze shield mark, c. 1890s, artist signed "Silvzen." 9½"; portrait of violinist, Bettlerin, cobalt and gold border. $1,000.00 – 1,200.00.

Close-up.

Royal Vienna style, underglaze shield mark, c. 1890s, signed "N. G. Max." 9½"; portrait of girl named Freude, dark green border with raised gold rose garlands. $1,000.00 – 1,200.00. (See mark #153.)

Royal Vienna style, underglaze shield mark, c. 1890s, artist signed "Tilz." 9½"; Art Nouveau–style border with heavy gold paste flowers, portrait of Ariadne. $1,400.00 – 1,500.00.

Close-up.

Close-up of border.

Royal Vienna style, overglaze shield mark, c. 1890s, artist signed "Siedel." 8"; cobalt and gold border, hand painting of lady straightening a bow for Cupid. $300.00 – 350.00.

Royal Vienna style, underglaze shield mark, c. 1870s. 9¼"; scene of partially clad lady in water with cupids, big fish in foreground; heavy gold border with beads and turquoise jewels. $500.00 – 600.00.

Close-up.

Royal Vienna style, underglaze shield mark, c. 1890s. 9¹/₂"; gold ground with raised gold leaves framed by an array of hand-painted green grape leaves; portrait of lovely lady named Epheu with long black hair and with garland of grape leaves in her hair, Art Nouveau. $1,400.00 – 1,500.00.

Royal Vienna style, underglaze shield mark, c. 1870s. Octagonal, 9³/₄"; "Amor's Revanche" in script and picture of Cupid trying to shoot his arrow at a young lady while her friends attempt to protect her from his advances, wonderful border with 16 different paintings in heavy gold and enameling. $1,000.00 – 1,200.00.

Close-up of border.

Close-up.

Royal Vienna style, Alexander Porcelain Works, E. Wahliss, c. 1894 – 1905, artist signed "F. A. Kaulbach." 9¾"; portrait of lovely lady, cobalt border with lavish gold. $1,100.00 – 1,200.00. (See mark #154.)

Close-up.

Royal Vienna style, Alexander Porcelain Works, E. Wahliss, c. 1905 – 1921. 9½"; fine painting of lady holding music and with a wreath of leaves on her head, cobalt blue border with white fleur-di-lis decoration. $950.00 – 1,100.00.

Close-up.

Royal Vienna style, underglaze shield mark, c. 1890s. 9½"; "Lerchenschlag" in script, hand-painted portrait of a wistful young woman, Tiffany burgundy luster on border with raised gold paste decorative cartouches. $1,300.00 – 1,500.00.

Royal Vienna style, underglaze shield mark, c. 1901 – 1910, artist signed "Ahne." 9½"; exceptionally well-painted portrait of President William McKinley by important porcelain and glass artist Joseph Ahne, raised gold border. $1,200.00 – 1,400.00.

Close-up.

Close-up.

Royal Vienna style, underglaze shield mark, c. 1901 – 1910, artist signed "Ahne." 9½"; exceptionally well-painted portrait of Spanish American War hero Admiral Winfield Schley (1839 – 1911) by important porcelain and glass artist Joseph Ahne, raised gold border. $1,200.00 – 1,400.00.

Royal Vienna style, underglaze shield mark, c. 1890s, artist signed "Wagner." 9½", marked "Erwartungsvoll" (anticipation); hand-painted portrait in center of lady looking out to sea and holding a single rose, intricate border with raised gold. $900.00 – 1,000.00.

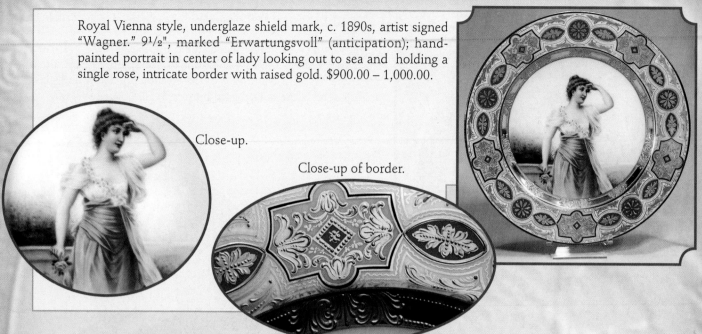

Close-up.

Close-up of border.

Royal Vienna style, underglaze shield mark, c. 1890s, artist signed "Greiner." 9⅓", marked "Gute Nacht" on bottom; portrait of lovely lady holding a candle, raised gold-beaded border. $1,200.00 – 1,400.00.

Close-up of border.

Close-up.

Royal Vienna style, red shield mark, c. 1890s, artist signed "Wagner." 9¼"; hand-painted portrait of coy lady with blonde hair, unusual gold border with hand-painted roses, entitled Sommerblumen, or "Summer Flowers." $1,200.00 – 1,500.00. (See mark #155.)

Royal Vienna style, c. 1890s. 7", in large ornate 16" bronze frame; allegorical scene. $500.00 – 600.00.

Royal Vienna blank, outside decorator, c. 1840s. 8"; hand-painted yellow rose, marked "Rosa Lutea" on back, pitting on gold band on border. $200.00 – 250.00.

Close-up.

P. J. Ulrich Studio, Vienna, c. 1890s. Majolica, 10¹/₂"; hand-painted portrait of a young boy with peacock-feathered hat. $500.00 – 600.00. (See mark #147.)

Unidentified Austrian Company, c. 1930s, signed "Ulrich."
10¼"; roses transfer. $45.00 – 60.00.

G. Mollik Company, Vienna, c. 1950s.
10"; mixed decoration of young boys.
$45.00 – 60.00.

Pirkenhammer (Fischer & Meig), c. 1920 – 1945. 9½"; excellent
hand-painted grapes and leaves. $400.00 – 450.00. (See mark #126.)

Pirkenhammer (Fischer & Meig), c. 1916 – 1918.
7¼"; rich cobalt blue ground, hand-painted birds,
insects, and flowering tree branches in gold and
bronze. $100.00 – 125.00. (See mark #127.)

Bing & Grondahl, c. 1958. Christmas plate, Santa Claus Coming by Kjeld Bonfils. $90.00 – 110.00.

Bing & Grondahl, c. 1960. Christmas plate, Danish Village Church. $135.00 – 200.00.

Bing & Grondahl, c. 1961. Christmas plate, Winter Harmony by Kjeld Bonfils. $75.00 – 95.00.

Royal Copenhagen, c. 1956. Christmas plate, Rosenborg Castle by Kai Lange, castle built by Christian IV in 1606. $165.00 – 225.00.

Royal Copenhagen, c. 1957. Christmas plate, The Good Shepherd by Hans H. Hansen. $120.00 – 130.00.

Royal Copenhagen, c. 1962. Christmas plate, The Little Mermaid by Kai Lange, based on the famous life-sized bronze inspired by Hans Christian Anderson. $200.00 – 300.00.

Royal Copenhagen, c. 1964. Christmas plate, Fetching the Christmas Tree by Kai Lange, horse-drawn sleighs still glide over snow-covered roads in Denmark at Christmas time. $60.00 – 90.00.

Royal Copenhagen, c. 1922 – present. 8½"; Blue Fluted Full Lace. $200.00 – 250.00. (See mark #133.)

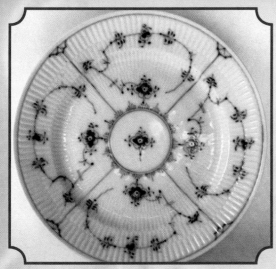

Royal Copenhagen, c. 1922 – present. 8"; Blue Fluted Plain. $40.00 – 50.00. (See mark #134.)

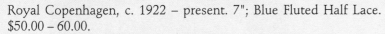

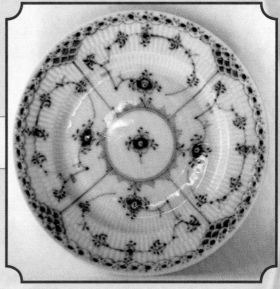

Royal Copenhagen, c. 1922 – present. 7"; Blue Fluted Half Lace. $50.00 – 60.00.

Royal Copenhagen, Flora Danica, c. 1960s. 9¼"; hand-painted yellow flowers, sawtooth gilt rim. $600.00 – 700.00.

Royal Copenhagen, Flora Danica, c. 1960s. 8½"; hand-painted purple flowers, sawtooth rim. $550.00 – 650.00. (See mark #135.)

Set of 12 service plates. Capodimonte style, c. 1890. 10½"; hand-painted Cupids in relief on border, hand-painted armorial crest in center. $2,500.00 – 3,000.00.

Plate from set above. $150.00– 200.00.

Plate from set at top. $150.00 – 200.00.

Plate from previous set. $150.00 – 200.00.

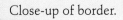

Close-up of border.

Close-up.

Capodimonte style, c. 1890, decorated by B. Block, Paris. Charger, 12½"; Cupids in relief on border, hand-painted flowers in center. $300.00 – 350.00.

Capodimonte style, c. 1890. 10½"; gold ground hand-painted flowers center, Cupids in relief on border. $200.00 – 275.00.

Capodimonte style, c. 1890 – 1920. 8¾"; hand-painted rose in center framed by gold, relief Cupids and figures in scenic setting on rim. $125.00 – 150.00. (See mark #12.)

Fornasetti, Milan, Italy, c. 1950. 10½"; decoupage fish applied to porcelain and lacquered. $200.00 – 250.00.

Maastricht (Petrus Regout), Holland, c. 1870. Earthenware, 8¼"; transfer scene of Timor. $75.00 – 100.00.

Delft, Holland, c. 1768. Earthenware, 9"; rare wedding plate, some rim chips. $500.00+.

Imperial Russia, St. Petersburg, c. 1881 – 1894. 9½"; decorated with hand-painted crown, Augustus monogram and gilt decoration. $500.00 – 600.00. (See mark #142.)

Close-up of border.

CHINA

EARLY DEVELOPMENT

The Chinese discovered how to make porcelain during the Tang Dynasty (618 – 907). They had a large supply of kaolin clay, which was the major ingredient. The Chinese developed kiln techniques and the glazing processes and created the white translucent body known as hard-paste porcelain.

During the Sung Dynasty (960 – 1278), porcelain production reached its highest point in terms of quality. The most important center of ceramic production was in the northern part of China, and white and celadon wares were the most famous. *Celadon* is a French term for the range of green colors, from deep olive green to a delicate sea green tint, produced in China.

In the Yuan Dynasty (1279 – 1368), Ching-te-chen became the center of porcelain production for the entire empire. Most of the porcelains had designs painted under the glaze in cobalt blue or copper red. The Imperial Porcelain Factory was established at Ching-te-chen at the beginning of the Ming Dynasty (1368 – 1644).

CHINESE EXPORT

Chinese Export porcelain dates back to the late eighteenth century, when it was introduced to the West by Portuguese traders from the East Indian Company. Porcelain manufacturing was still at the city of Ching-te-chen. The population was more than one million, and 3,000 kilns were in operation. Much of the porcelain was sent to Canton, where it was big business to decorate porcelain items for export to Europe and America.

The lovely Chinese porcelain was immediately successful in Europe and America. Especially sought after by collectors are items in the Famille Rose (pink palette) patterns. A few of the patterns include Rose Medallion, Rose Canton, Rose Mandarin, 100 Butterflies, and Tobacco Leaf. Rose Canton contains reserves of birds, butterflies, and flowers.

Chinese Export ware had three major design elements in the eighteenth century: Oriental motifs, designs adapted from European prints, and armorials. Armorials were coats-of-arms of important European and American families. Armorial plates were very popular in the eighteenth century, and there are nearly 3,000 known armorial service patterns.

Chinese Famille Rose plate with Seven Borders, Yung Cheng period (1723 – 1735), British Museum, C120, printed by Waterlow & Sons Ltd.

C. 120. "Famille rose" Plate with Seven Borders. D. 8·25"
Yung Chêng period (1723-35).
British Museum. Printed by Waterlow & Sons Limited.

 ## JAPAN

EARLY DEVELOPMENT

The earliest ceramic art in Japan was a black coiled pottery known as Joman ware, made over 2,000 years ago. In the early thirteenth century, Kato Shirozayemon went to China to study the art of pottery, especially how to produce black-glazed tea bowls, which were valued by the Japanese for use in their tea ceremony. On his return, Shirozayemon started to make similar bowls.

In the sixteenth century, the victorious master Hideyoshi returned to Japan from Korea, bringing potters with

him. They settled at a number of areas like Kyoto, Karatsu, and Satsuma and started to produce wares in current Korean styles.

A Korean potter named Ameya developed a popular type of tea bowl around 1525. He was awarded a gold seal from Hideyoshi engraved with the word *raku*, which means "enjoyment." The manufacturing of rakuware spread widely. Rakuware was earthenware fired at a low temperature on a hearth and covered with a treacle-type glaze.

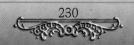

The art of porcelain making was brought to Japan from China by Shonsui in the first half of the sixteenth century. The first kilns were established in the early decades of the seventeenth century at Arita. The first wares were produced in underglaze blue. Soon large quantities were shipped to Holland.

Ceramic techniques continued to develop during the next three centuries in Japan. Entire families worked in the pottery centers, passing their skills down to their children.

Following the reopening of trade with Japan by Commodore Perry of the United States in 1853, Japanese pottery and porcelain became extremely popular, attracting the attention of collectors. During the last quarter of the nineteenth century, the Japanese influence played an important part in the Art Nouveau movement.

A porcelain shop in Japan, postcard, the Ratograph Co., NY (Germany).

IMARI

Imari is the most famous name in Japanese porcelain. It was first produced in the seventeenth century in the secluded mountain villages in the Arita district of the southern Japanese island of Kyushu and was guarded by samurai warriors to protect the secret ingredients. The earliest Imari was the blue and white ware called Arita. The clay had a high iron content, making it good for firing at a high temperature. The finished products from the Arita district were often shipped through the port of Imari, from whence came the name.

At the end of the seventeeth century, overglaze red was introduced, and it rapidly grew in popularity. During the nineteenth century, enamel decoration in multiple colors was popular among the wealthy Japanese, who were the main buyers of expensive porcelain. Five colors — cobalt blue, pale blue, iron red, green, and gold — dominated. The complexity of design increased during the nineteenth century, and the ware became known as *nishikide* Imari, or "brocade." Floral decorations dominate the center decorations, and the border patterns are derived from textiles.

Imari chargers are popular items with collectors today. A large charger (14½") dating from the nineteenth century could easily bring $1,800.00 – 2,000.00.

Three Japanese plates with cute kittens, postcard, Raphael Tuck & Sons #6495.

FUKAGAWA

In Arita, many families of ceramic artists participated in the production of traditional porcelain items intended for the Japanese domestic market. One such important group is the Fukagawa family, which has had porcelain kilns on the side of a mountain in Arita since the 1650s. One descendant, Chuji Fukagawa, founded the Fukagawa Porcelain Manufacturing Company in 1894 to produce industrial ceramics and high-quality tableware. His first imports to the West occurred in 1900, when Fukagawa was awarded the Gold Medal of Honor at the International Exposition in Paris. The Fukagawa Company continues to produce top-quality tableware today.

KUTANI

Kutani means "nine valleys," and wares with this name were first produced in the middle of the seventeenth century in a remote village in the Kaga province of Kutani. Kutani is distinguished by the use of five bold colors, red, deep blue, deep yellow, purple, and green. The entire surface of the item is covered with colorful decoration. Themes include birds and flowers, landscape motifs, and geometric patterns. There are rarely seals on the bases of Kutani wares; however, the characters for Kutani, as well as the names of the artists, often appear.

Kutani ware was unknown in the West until a group of the pieces were displayed at the Paris Exhibition of 1867. Here the red, gold, and soft white tones were greatly admired. Soon a wide variety of items, such as plates, vases, and tea wares, began to be produced for both domestic and foreign markets. Pieces have white backgrounds and eggshell-thin bodies. Kutani kilns are still producing porcelain for export.

NIPPON

Nippon identifies wares made in Japan from 1891 to 1921, rather than a single maker. After 1921, the word *Japan* was used. Nippon porcelain is highly collectible today and can be found with many different designs and methods of manufacture. Many pieces are hand painted, and it is hard to find two pieces exactly alike.

At least 300 kilns operated in Honshu, Kyushu, Skikoku, and other provinces in the nineteenth century in Japan. Whole villages made porcelain and decorated it. Children were often used to help decorate Nippon. A tremendous amount of Nippon was exported to the United States, and there is a significant difference in quality.

There are many types of decoration on Nippon. Gold was used quite lavishly on pieces exported before 1912. Gold overlay pieces are very desirable and bring the highest prices. Some top-quality Nippon items have heavy gold on a cobalt blue ground. The gold was not very durable, and today a number of these pieces have considerable gilt wear.

Cobalt items were made with oxidized cobalt blue coloring. Originally gosu, a pebble found in Japanese river beds, was used for cobalt coloring. Gosu became too scarce and expensive, and in the 1860s oxidized cobalt was imported into Japan and used in its place. Nippon with cobalt and gold is extremely desirable to collectors.

Beading is another decorative technique used on many pieces of Nippon. Beading is a series of dots of clay slip which were painted in a number of colors, especially gold and brown. Beading was used on rims and around floral and scenic cartouches.

Nippon plates are very popular with collectors. Cake plates are readily available and are often hand painted with colorful roses overlaid with gold beading. Some of the most desirable plates have blown out decoration, portrait transfers, or hand painted scenes.

PHOENIX BIRD CHINA

Blue and white Phoenix Bird china has been produced by various Japanese potteries from the late nineteenth century to the 1970s. With slight variations, the design features the phoenix and scroll-like vines. The phoenix is adapted from Chinese art and is a bird of paradise who lives on earth. It is associated with the Empress of Japan, so it is the symbol of all that's beautiful.

The pattern is usually a transfer print, with the body of the phoenix facing forward and the head facing backwards over its wings. There are at least four spots on his chest, and his wings spread up and out. Most borders have a cloud and mountain motif.

The first Phoenix Bird china was marked "Nippon" and was sold from 1891 to 1921. From the 1920s to the 1940s, Phoenix Bird china was mainly sold by discounts stores, such as Woolworth's, or sold wholesale through catalogs from the Morimura Brothers in Japan. Phoenix Bird china was also given away as premiums by a number of companies.

Phoenix Bird collector and expert Joan Oates has written five books identifying the hundreds of different patterns, shapes, and sizes of Phoenix Bird chinaware and variations, such as Flying Turkey and Flying Dragon. Phoenix Bird china is attractive and reasonably priced. There is a tremendous variety of patterns and styles for collectors to choose from.

SATSUMA

Japan has produced some of the world's most beautiful ceramic art, and Satsuma is one of the most distinctive. Resembling aged ivory, Satsuma is a soft-paste porcelain, characterized by a fine creamy crackle glaze. The finely detailed hand painting and gold enameling is what makes Satsuma so treasured and sought after by discriminating collectors throughout the world.

Near the end of the sixteenth century, Shimazu Yoshihiro, a general in the Japanese army, invaded Korea as a first step to conquering the Chinese empire. After several years of victorious fighting, the Japanese army was summoned home by its shogun. Yoshihiro brought 17 to 20 Korean potters and their families home with him. Grateful that their lives were spared, the potters introduced their art of ceramics to the Japanese. Some of the immigrant potters settled in the Satsuma province and built their kilns on a hill, just like they did at home in Korea.

This early Satsuma ware was made from an excellent local clay with the addition of feldspar and some wood ash. The clay was found in nearby hills and mountains near some volcanic hot springs, and that was the reason it was so rich. The earliest Satsuma wares were in red or reddish brown paste and covered with a transparent glaze.

Satsuma was made continuously during the next two centuries. By the nineteenth century, potteries were set up in five major locations: Kagoshima, Kyoto at Awata, the island of Awaji, Yokohama, and Tokyo.

At the London International Exhibition in 1862, Satsuma was displayed in a Western country for the first time. From its first appearance, it was well received and in demand. When Satsuma became a popular export, the styles changed to suit Western tastes. Pieces became larger, and more colors were added. To satisfy Victorian tastes, raised enameling was used frequently in the decoration.

After World War I, Japan began exporting large quantities of Satsuma to the West. Many pieces had their entire surfaces enameled. In the 1920s, a matte black background was popular. In the 1930s, red and brown were predominant background colors. The mass-produced Satsuma wares of the 1920s through the 1940s had colorful and vivid decoration, but the overall quality of such pieces is somewhat sloppy and coarse.

Most pieces of early nineteenth century Satsuma are decorated with scenes from nature. The Japanese people love trees and flowers and represent them in much of their art. The cherry tree, treasured in Japan for its blossoms even more than for its fruit, is often featured on Satsuma wares. The cherry blossom is the national flower of Japan and the name for it means "faithful warrior."

Favorite flower themes on Satsuma ware include the lotus and the king of flowers, the peony, which is the symbol of summer. The iris is much loved by the Japanese because it is said to ward off evil spirits and illness. The chrysanthemum is often featured on Satsuma pieces and represents longevity or good health because the flower blooms late in the year and lives longer than other flowers. The chrysanthemum is on the crest of the emperor of Japan.

Birds and animals have always been a part of Oriental art. Peacocks symbolize elegance and good fortune, and the crane stands for good luck and longevity. Mythical beasts are also featured in Satsuma ware. The dragon is the most loved of all mythical beasts and is said to reside in the sky. Dragons are usually painted with lightning, clouds, water, or flames.

In the middle of the nineteenth century, human figures appeared on Satsuma ware, and these were often in the forms of warriors (samurai), theatrical characters, and legendary heroes. The seven lucky gods were a popular subject and were portrayed with their attributes. Women are seen in domestic pursuits and are often portrayed with their children. Rakan are sages endowed with supernatural powers and appear emaciated or austere. They are often portrayed with their halos. The rakan and dragon were used extensively on Satsuma wares made between the wars.

The decoration of Satsuma ware has several distinct characteristics. The crackle glaze is the most important, enhancing the piece by producing a play of light on the surface. On later wares the crackle is large with long, irregular lines.

By the late eighteenth century, a nishikide design was used. Masses of polychromed floral enameling covering almost the entire surface of the object gave the piece a brocade effect.

Several types of relief decoration are often found on Satsuma ware. Moriage is applied slip decoration in which the motif is formed by hand and applied to the bisque. Applying a slip-trailed motif involves trailing liquefied clay though a tube onto the bisque, similar to using our cake-decorating techniques. A dramatic decoration appealing to Western tastes is the dragon scale. Globules of gray or white enamel are made to represent dragon or serpent scales and are usually laid on a dark background.

The marks on Satsuma ware can be very confusing. Some marks are of individual potters while others include marks of the factory or of the individuals who order quantities of the ware for their own use or for gifts. Seals and other familiar Japanese characters were also used for marks. It is not really necessary to worry about the marks to enjoy a collection of Satsuma plates. Select pieces that are pleasing to you and are the best quality you can afford.

Satsuma kilns are still operating today, and wares are being exported. Vases, plates, and tea sets are popular. There are several differences between the old and new. The potting today is mechanical instead of by hand. The enamels are not as textured. The gold is thinly applied and is not as bright, and the crackle is not as fine. The two most predominant patterns are Mille Fleur (1,000 flowers) and A Thousand Flying Cranes. Colors are more vivid, and red, bright blue, and green are accented with white, black, and a touch of gold. The new pieces are beautiful and expensive but are not yet antiques.

Canton, c. 1860 – 1880. 5"; hand-painted village scene. $60.00 – 80.00.

Famille Rose, c. 1890s. 9³/₄"; 100 Butterflies pattern. $200.00 – 250.00.

Famille Rose, c. 1840s. 9¹/₂"; Black Butterfly pattern. $350.00 – 400.00.

Rose Canton, c. 1830 – 1840. 7¹/₂"; intricate butterfly, bird, and flower design. $250.00 – 300.00.

Rose Medallion, c. 1850s. 8¹/₂". $200.00 – 250.00.

Rose Canton, c. 1840. Celadon shrimp dish, 11"; hand-enameled birds, insects, and flowers. $750.00 – 800.00.

Arita, c. 1890s. Blue and white charger, 16¼"; transfer scene with Oriental figures. $400.00 — 500.00.

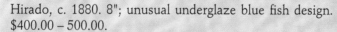

Fukagawa, c. 1880. Charger, 18"; rare trout painting. $2,500.00 – 3,000.00.

Hirado, c. 1880. 8"; unusual underglaze blue fish design. $400.00 – 500.00.

Imari, c. 1830 – 1850. Diamond-shaped, 6"; unusual fan and floral design. $200.00 – 225.00.

Imari, c. 1880s. Scalloped charger, 12"; vivid red, blue, and gold decoration. $750.00 – 800.00.

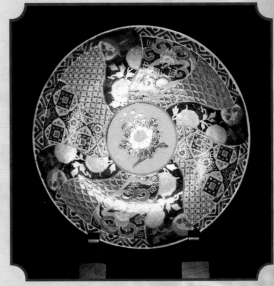

Imari, c. 1870 – 1880. Charger, 15"; swirling brocade pattern. $1,000.00 – 1,200.00.

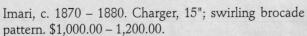

Imari, c. 1870 – 1890. 7$\frac{1}{2}$"; village scenes. $300.00 – 400.00.

Imari, c. 1870 – 1890. 7$\frac{1}{2}$"; iris and insect. $250.00 – 300.00.

Imari, c. 1860 – 1890. 8"; blue and white bird and flowering branch design. $250.00 – 300.00.

Imari, c. 1890 – 1900. Scalloped platter; flowers in pot design. $500.00 – 600.00.

Imari, c. 1880s. Charger, 18"; intricate pattern. $1,400.00 – 1,600.00.

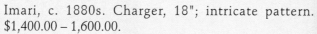

Imari, c. 1890 – 1920. Scalloped square dish or plate, 11⅝"; hand-painted flowerpot design. $300.00 – 325.00.

Kutani, c. 1890s. Heavy earthenware plate, 9¹/₂"; medallions of hand-painted figures, birds, and flowers. $250.00 – 300.00. (See mark #61.)

Kutani on Satsuma blank, c. 1870s. Charger, 15¹/₂"; scene of lohans. $2,200.00 – 2,300.00.

Kutani, c. 1890 – 1910. 7"; lake scene. $150.00 – 200.00.

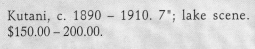

Kutani, c. 1890 – 1910. Tray; elaborate scenes and figures with lavish gold. $1,800.00 – 2,000.00.

Nabeshima, c. 1780 – 1820. Dish, 5½"; rare blue and white blossom design. $2,000.00 – 2,500.00.

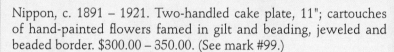

Nippon, c. 1891 – 1921. Two-handled cake plate, 11"; cartouches of hand-painted flowers famed in gilt and beading, jeweled and beaded border. $300.00 – 350.00. (See mark #99.)

Nippon, c. 1891 – 1921. Octagonal cake plate, 10"; black matte border with heavy gold flowers, hand-painted peach roses and grapes. $350.00 – 400.00. (See mark #100.)

Close-up.

Nippon, c. 1891 – 1921, unmarked. 10"; rich cobalt ground with elaborate gilt stylized flowers and beads. $300.00 – 350.00.

Nippon, c. 1891 – 1921, unmarked. Scalloped, 7"; center cartouche of pink hand-painted roses, cobalt border, five rose medallions, lavish gilt and beads. $100.00 – 125.00.

Nippon, c. 1891 – 1921. 9³/4"; gold ground overlaid with gold beading, cartouches with hand-painted roses. $300.00 – 350.00.

Nippon, c. 1891 – 1921. 9³/₄"; center transfer portrait of Queen Louise, apple green ground with coral and emerald jeweling and gold beads. $1,200.00 – 1,400.00. (See mark #101.)

Close-up.

Close-up of border.

Nippon, c. 1891 – 1921. 8²/₃"; hand-painted ducks in a pond, gold stars and beads on border. $400.00 – 450.00.

Nippon, c. 1891 – 1921. 9¹/₄"; eight gold cartouches with three hand-painted roses inside, framed by gold beads, lavish gold overlay. $400.00 – 500.00.

Nippon, c. 1891 – 1921. 10"; lush pink hand-painted roses in full bloom with buds, gold and brown border, gold beading. $250.00 – 300.00.

Nippon, c. 1891 – 1921. 9"; three hand-painted roses in center, apple green border with floral cartouches alternating with gold vermicelli reserves. $250.00 – 300.00.

Nippon, c. 1891 – 1921. 10"; eight hand-painted roses on gold beaded border and rose in center, cobalt rim. $350.00 – 400.00.

Close-up of center.

Nippon, c. 1891 – 1921. 9"; hand-painted lake scene. $125.00 – 150.00.

Nippon, c. 1891 – 1921. 10½"; hand-painted forest scene with two deer standing on a hill, lavish gold and beaded cobalt border. $400.00 – 450.00.

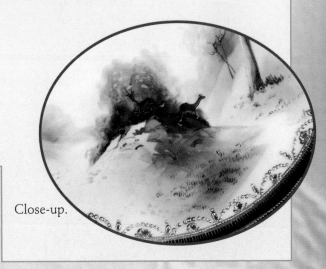

Close-up.

Noritake, c. 1930s. Charger, 12"; Howo pattern. $95.00 – 125.00.

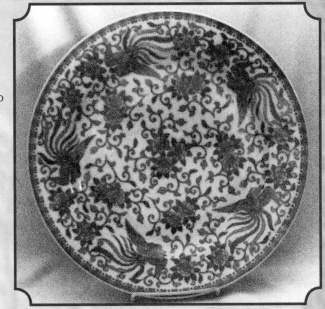

Noritake, c. 1930s. Charger, 11¾"; Twin Phoenix pattern on border. $95.00 – 125.00.

Noritake, c. 1908 – 1911. 9"; hand-painted fish. Cream border with gilt decoration. $175.00 – 200.00. (See mark #102.)

Phoenix Bird, c. 1920 – 1930s. Charger, 11½".
$150.00 – 175.00.

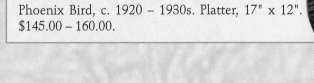

Phoenix Bird, c. 1920 – 1930s. Platter, 17" x 12".
$145.00 – 160.00.

Phoenix Bird, c. 1920 – 1930s. Platter, 16" x 10½"; left phoenix is upside down, decal reversed. $150.00 – 165.00.

Flying Turkey, c. 1920 – 1930s, hand-painted mark in Japanese characters. Platter, 14$\frac{1}{2}$" x 11". $125.00 – 140.00.

Flying Turkey, c. 1920 – 1930s. Platter, 12$\frac{1}{2}$" x 8$\frac{1}{2}$"; heartlike border, transfer print. $65.00 – 75.00.

Flying Dragon, c. 1920 – 1930s. 8$\frac{1}{2}$"; green and white. $45.00 – 55.00.

Satsuma, c. 1870 – 1880. Charger, 14$\frac{1}{2}$"; hand-painted lohans. $2,000.00 – 2,500.00.

Satsuma, c. 1870. Scalloped; celebration of Boy's Day Festival. $800.00 – 1,000.00.

Satsuma, c. 1890. 8½"; procession scene, artist Dozan. $3,000.00 – 3,500.00.

Studio ware, c. 1920s. 6"; moriage-style iris. $500.00 – 600.00.

Made in Japan, c. 1920 – 1930. Scalloped majolica, 8½"; maple-leaf design. $50.00 – 75.00.

KNOWLEDGE

Knowledge is a key that will open many doors for you. Books, magazines, trade papers, and auction catalogs are useful tools. Many excellent books can be found in our bibliography. Talking to antique dealers and fellow collectors will help you make good decisions in your buying. Take advantage of their experience and knowledge of the subject.

Another helpful source of information on plates is your computer. Search for "plates" and you will be amazed at what you will find.

If you have an interest in collecting plates and you are willing to do a small amount of research on the subject, you should be able to make some good buys and keep adding to your collection. Knowledge will help you know the difference between authentic pieces and reproductions. Knowledge will also help you to know the difference between old plates and plates currently being made, and will allow you to know the values of both.

AVAILABILITY

Plates can be found at antique shows and in shops. At these places, you will have the opportunity to talk to dealers and ask questions about the items.

Auctions are a good source to use when adding to your plate collection. Preview the item carefully for flaws and damages. Remember, it is the buyer's responsibility to check the condition of an item. You must also consider the buyer's premium in figuring a bid price you are willing to pay. Above all, don't get caught up in auction fever. Determine how much you are willing to pay and stop there.

INTERNET BUYING

An exciting new source for finding and buying antiques is the Internet. There are many advantages to using this method. You can shop the whole world from the comfort of your home, and you can keep all your reference materials handy. You may also find some rare and unusual pieces.

The Internet also has some disadvantages. Not being able to have a "hands on" inspection is certainly one of the biggest problems you'll have. Buying from a photograph and a brief description has significantly changed the way we buy and sell antiques.

You can ask questions, but the seller may not be able to answer them properly. The seller sometimes does not have a good knowledge of what is being sold and finds it hard to exactly describe the item. You may have to read between the lines and ask detailed questions. Many sellers are not trained to recognize hairlines, chips, or missing gilt and do not understand what an incised mark is or how to date a piece properly.

You must be very careful to read the fine print and understand all the conditions described. There are times that an item is sold as is and cannot be returned. When buying on the Internet, you should know what the seller's return policy is. If bidding in an auction, always ask all your questions before bidding.

Inspect an item you receive as a result of your Internet buying as soon as you take it out of the box. Some sellers only have a three-day return policy. Occasionally, rare items have been restored. A black light is a valuable tool to help you discover if an item has been restored. Run your fingers over the piece and feel it for chips and cracks.

Receiving items with hairline cracks and chips is a major problem. Some sellers don't see hairlines, as they can be easy to miss. This is why you should tap every piece of porcelain you buy to see if it rings and also have a good jeweler's loupe. Always inspect a piece you get though the mail in a well-lighted area.

If something is not just right, inform the person you received it from right away and say you want to return it. A reputable dealer will refund your purchase price without any questions asked.

With any fine porcelain plate, condition is very important. Almost all plates have been handled and used, and therefore, can be prone to small chips, hairline cracks, or wear to the paint or gilt. Some may even have some repairs or restorations.

Most chips appear on the rims of plates. A chip on a plate happens when it is hit by a hard object. The best way to detect a chip is to physically look for one and to use your fingers to feel for one. A chip can be restored by a professional, but it's an expensive process and hard to do. If the item is rare, it may pay to have it restored.

Hairline cracks are sometimes hard to detect. A good test is to hold the piece by your fingertips and tap it with a finger of your other hand; it should ring like a bell. If it thuds, there is something wrong and you should examine the piece very carefully. It is almost impossible to remove a fine hairline crack from a plate, although a small chip may be repairable.

Crazing is tiny surface cracks caused by shrinking or other technical defects in the glaze. Wares may be crazed in the kiln if the body expands or contracts at a different rate than the glaze. Some of the early kilns were heated by different fuels, and it became hard to maintain a constant temperature. Today kilns are all temperature controlled and crazing is not so common.

Crazing could take away from the appearance of piece and also make it susceptible to a hairline crack. Crazing is hard to detect and often is not visible to the naked eye. A good test for crazing is to use the tap, tap method with your finger. If the piece thuds or just rings slightly, that is a good sign that it may have some crazing. If it rings like a bell, you can be almost sure that there is no crazing. If you see staining on a plate which can't be removed with soap and water, the piece is probably crazed.

Some of the most beautiful late-nineteenth- and early-twentieth-century English bone china plates made by Coalport, Royal Worcester, Minton, and Carlton Ware had problems with crazing. Sometimes the crazing was just on the bottom of the plate. A small amount of crazing should not deter you from buying a piece that has beautiful workmanship, such as jeweling or fine hand painting.

Most collectors expect a small amount of gilt wear. If it is excessive, however, it could take away from a piece's appearance, value, or both.

Collecting restored pieces may not hurt your collection, and you might be able to buy a rare plate at a reasonable price. A poor restoration can normally be detected. Look for a difference in color or thickness, or an unevenness in the porcelain. If the piece is for your own collection and it looks acceptable to you, that's all that matters.

As a rule of thumb, washing a plate should be done by hand rather than in a dishwasher. The detergents used in dishwashers are very harsh, and the high heat in the drying cycle can cause damage to the gilt. Never use a dishwasher to wash a fine hand-painted cabinet plate. If a piece is to be cleaned and it does not have any restorations, you may soak it in some lukewarm water and may use a mild detergent; then rinse the piece and let it dry naturally, or gently pat it dry with a soft towel.

Little girl washing an old plate, postcard, N. R. M.

A cabinet plate is much safer if it is displayed in a closed case or cabinet. It is less likely to be touched or moved, and it will not collect dust or grease as much as an exposed piece. Pieces in cabinets will eventually need cleanings, however.

When buying a plate an important factor to consider is the quality of the piece. Are the colors vivid and pleasing to the eye? If a piece is signed by the artist, it will usually be more valuable, although not all artists are considered equal.

🌼 RECORD KEEPING 🌼

Keeping good records is very important. You should know what price you paid for each plate as you add it to your collection. Should you decide to sell your collection, this information will be useful. After each purchase, write a little note as to where the piece was purchased and when, who sold it to you, and for how much. Over the years, as your plate collection increases, you will have all the information on hand. You can also include historical facts about the item, such as the artist's name, the period of time when the piece was produced, its age, its style, and its condition. This information can easily be recorded today on a personal computer.

Another good policy is to photograph your plate collection as a method of record keeping. This will also give you a picture of your collection for insurance purposes. And if you want to to show your pieces off to fellow collectors, it is much easier to carry a picture around than it is to carry your pieces around. It helps you if you want to trade for pieces you don't have.

Suzette

Cat showing off her plate, postcard A. & M. B. #209.

🌼 PROTECTION 🌼

As your plate collection increases and, hopefully, becomes more valuable, you should consider insurance for it. Just think what your loss would be if there were a fire or theft. Nothing would be covered if you didn't have fine arts coverage added to your homeowner's insurance policy. If your insurance company requires an outside appraiser, you should hire a qualified person with recognized credentials. Look for one in your local telephone directory. Look under "Appraisers" or "Antique Dealers." You may also be able to get a recommendation from an antique dealer or your insurance company. It's another good reason to photograph your entire collection.

DISPLAY

Your decorative plate collection will enhance the décor of your home when properly displayed. As porcelain plates are fragile, they are best displayed in glass-enclosed curio cabinets. Never store fine porcelain in very hot or cold locations, as any sudden changes in temperature could possibly crack the glaze.

You may want to buy plate stands or hangers to display your plate collection. They are available in a wide assortment of styles and configurations to suite your taste. They can be purchased at antique shows, on the Internet, or at a local gift shops or hardware stores.

Remember to keep your precious plate collection out of reach of small children and pets. If you use a cleaning service, point out your fragile pieces to the cleaners. It is probably best to clean your collection yourself.

Plate display, courtesy of collector Brenda Pardee.

Plate display, courtesy of collector Brenda Pardee.

Christmas plate display, courtesy of collector Mary Davis.

Limoges bird plate display, author's collection.

The rarer and more valuable the antique, the more likely it will be reproduced. Good quality Royal Vienna style and Dresden portrait plates have always been desirable, and prices are high today. We are beginning to see new reproductions on the Internet today, and several are very well done.

We have seen two examples that were sold by the same German dealer. We believe they were decorated in Russia. The first portrays a beautiful nude. It had a fake shield mark, and the maker's mark was covered with a gold flower. When the gold flower was removed, we found the blank was made by the Furstenberg Company, Germany, dating 1975 to the present. The nude is completely hand painted, and the plate is artist signed on the front. The border is done extremely well with raised gilt decoration. To the untrained eye, this plate could easily pass for a late nineteenth century Royal Vienna–style plate.

Close-up.

you know that they are quite new. Good-quality Royal Vienna–style and Dresden portrait plates are selling in the $1,000.00 – 1,600.00 price range today. We would put a $500.00 price tag on each of these plates.

Royal Vienna style, shield mark, Furstenberg blank, c. 1975 – present, artist signed "Reimer." 10"; hand-painted nude woman with long flowing hair, miniature painting of six nudes on the bottom right, finely gilded and beaded border. $500.00 – 600.00.

Reproduction, Dresden, fake Richard Klemm mark, c. 1975 – present. 9$\frac{1}{2}$"; hand-painted portrait of man and woman, heavy gilt on border, nice quality. $300.00 – 350.00.

Another plate has a fake Richard Klemm, Dresden mark. It also has a gold flower, covering the maker. The plate is quite beautiful with an inset of two hand-painted portraits. It's interesting that Richard Klemm did several plates with inset portraits. It is artist signed. Again, the raised gilt border is stunning.

There is nothing wrong with buying these plates for your collection, as they are well painted, as long as

Close-up.

Phony mark.

There are some large chargers with a phony Sevres mark being reproduced today. They are very well done, and it is difficult to tell that they are not hand painted. One of the subjects found features Napoleon crowning Josephine.

Charger. Reproduction, phony Sevres mark, signed "David, Current." Charger, 11½"; "Napoleon 1st couronnant Josephine" written on back, mixed decoration. $200.00 – 300.00.

USEFUL INFORMATION

DELFT CHARGERS

There are a number of "Delft"-style charger reproductions signed "Boch Freres." They were first made in the 1960s and 1970s. These new Delft chargers have been sold in antique reproduction stores for over 30 years and have been popular sellers. They cost about $16.00 wholesale and have been seen priced from $35.00 to $50.00 at flea markets and up to $500.00 at antique shows. The true Boch Freres Company, located in Louviere, Belgium, made many kinds of ceramics, including art pottery and hand-painted tin-glazed delftware in both blue and white and polychrome. By 1920, Boch stopped producing hand-painted delftware.

Charger. Reproduction, Delft style, marked Boch and Delft, c. 1950s – present. Charger, 15¾", transfer of man and woman pulled by horse and carriage, blue and white. $35.00 – 50.00.

Phony mark.

Charger. Reproduction, Delft style, marked Boch and Delft, c. 1950s – present. Charger, 15¾", Delft style blue and white scene. $35.00 – 50.00.

OYSTER PLATES

The prices of oyster plates have soared during the last few years, and it was predictable that reproductions would come into the marketplace. There are a number of porcelain oyster plates that have been copied. Nippon reproduced oyster plates are turning up all over and can be found from coast to coast. The fake pieces even have a Nippon mark under the glaze. Some examples of phony Nippon oyster plates being sold by a reproduction outlet today are as follows: a 9" oyster plate with floral decoration inside each of the six wells, marked "Nippon," sells for $12.00; a four-well oyster-shaped plate with a center sauce well, measuring 8½", can be bought wholesale for $15.00; and a 9" white oyster plate with six wells and a smaller center well for a lemon, molded in the star design, is priced at $12.00.

The popular unmarked napkin oyster plate with four oyster-shaped wells and petal-shaped sauce well, superimposed on a molded napkin, has been reproduced, according to a recent issue of the *Oyster Plate and Collectibles Society International Newsletter.* The copy is easy to distinguish because of the Haviland logo forgery, as the Haviland Company did not produce the original plate. The back of the rim also has two wire loops embedded where a wire could be threaded in order to hang the plate on the wall. The reproduction is exceptionally heavy, and the logo and embedded wire loops are dead giveaways. Most of the authentic napkin oyster plates are unmarked.

An oyster plate ostensibly made by the Haviland Company has recently turned up at antique shows and shops. The Haviland mark for the period between 1876 and 1889 is printed on the back of the plate in large black letters. Anyone who has handled the delicate and translucent china made by Haviland will not be fooled by this reproduction. The porcelain is rather heavy and coarse, and the hand painting is amateurish. The back of the plate has runny glaze that was sloppily applied.

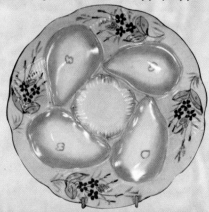

Oyster plate. Reproduction, phony Haviland mark, c. 1980s: heavy porcelain with amateurish hand painting.

Another porcelain oyster plate that is frequently seen in the marketplace is suspicious. The plate has a wheel-spoke design with six wells between the spokes. A rather crude oyster is hand painted in each well. It is believed this oyster plate was produced about 30 years ago as a Haviland copy.

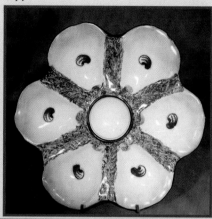

Oyster plate. Suspicious, heavy porcelain, possibly reproduced about 30 years ago.

In *Oyster Plates,* the Karsnitzes report that Union Porcelain Works oyster plates are being reproduced today with a much larger mark than the originals. It is stamped with black ink and can easily be recognized.

Some of the French companies making new oyster plates today are Sarreguemines, Longchamp, and Quimper. In a recent Quimper catalog, a new oyster platter is shown in the Décor Henriot pattern. It is 13" with 12 oyster-shaped wells that have floral decoration. A Breton woman is painted in the center well: This platter retails for $150.00. A 9¾" oyster plate in the same pattern has six wells with flowers, and a peasant man in the center well. It sells for $79.50.

The best advice for collectors is to know your dealer and gain experience handling as many oyster plates as possible. When buying an oyster plate, there are certain guidelines to keep in mind:

1. Is the porcelain of a fine, delicate quality?
2. Is the glaze smooth and evenly coated?
3. Are there signs of age, such as crazing, wear on the bottom, scratch marks, and faded gilding?
4. Are the colors vivid?
5. Is the hand painting professionally done?
6. Are the marks valid?

When buying an oyster plate, be cautious, and if there is a doubt in your mind, don't buy it. Remember, experience is your best teacher.

1. Aynsley, c. 1930 – 1950.

2. Aynsley, c. 1891– 1920.

3. Bawo & Dotter, Austria, c. 1884 – 1914, made for Higgins & Setzer.

4. Belleek Pottery Co., David McBirney & Co., c. 1980 – 1989.

5. Belleek Pottery Co., David McBirney & Co., c. 1921 – 1954.

6. Bishop & Stonier, c. 1891 – 1936.

7. Bodley, c. 1875 – 1892.

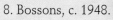

8. Bossons, c. 1948.

9. Brownfield, William & Son, c. 1871 – 1876.

10. Brown-Westhead, c. 1880 – 1890, made for Davis Collamore & Co., NY.

11. Burgess & Leigh, c. 1930s.

12. Capodimonte style, c. 1890 – 1920.

13. Cauldon Co., c. 1905 – 1920.

14. Challinor, E. & Co., c. 1853 – 1862.

15. Coalport, c. 1891 – 1920, made for D. B. Bedell & Co., NY.

16. Coalport, c. 1939 – 1959.

17. Coalport, c. 1881 – 1890, made for Daniell & Co., London.

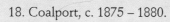

18. Coalport, c. 1875 – 1880.

19. Coalport, c. 1960 – present.

20. Coalport, c. 1820 – 1825, rare Feltspar mark.

21. Columbian Art Co., c. 1893 – 1902.

22. Copeland Spode, c. 1891 – 1920, made for Tiffany & Co., NY.

23. Copeland Spode, c. 1851 – 1885.

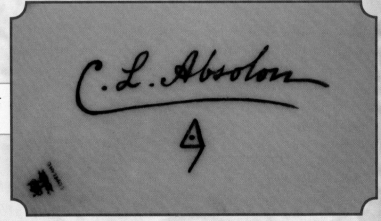

24. Copeland Spode, c. 1851 – 1885, amateur decoration.

25. Copeland Spode, c. 1883.

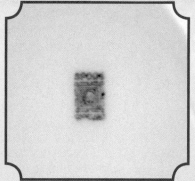

26. Copeland Spode, c. 1875 – 1890.

27. Copeland Spode, c. 1891 (special jeweled porcelain mark).

28. Crown Derby, c. 1878 – 1890.

29. Doulton Burslem, c. 1881 – 1890 (registry mark dates 1887).

30. Royal Doulton, c. 1930s, made for Ovington Bros., NY.

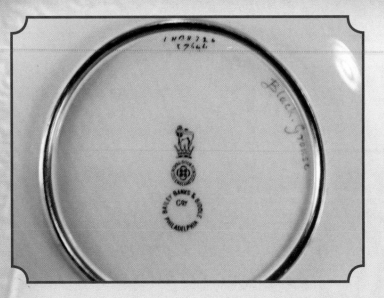

31. Royal Doulton, c. 1910 – 1915, made for Bailey, Banks & Biddle, Philadelphia, PA.

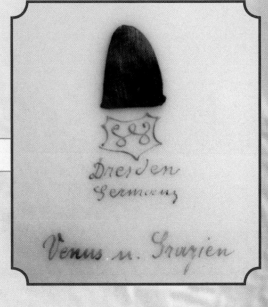

32. Dresden, R. Wehsner, c. 1895 – 1918.

33. Dresden, R. Klemm, c. 1890 – 1916.

34. Dresden, R. Klemm, c. 1900 – 1920.

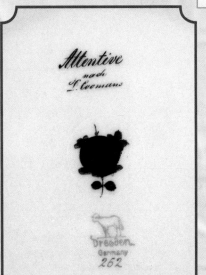

35. Dresden, Ambrosius Lamm, c. 1891 – 1914.

36. Dresden, Franziska Hirsch, c. 1910 – 1920, made for Ovington Bros., NY.

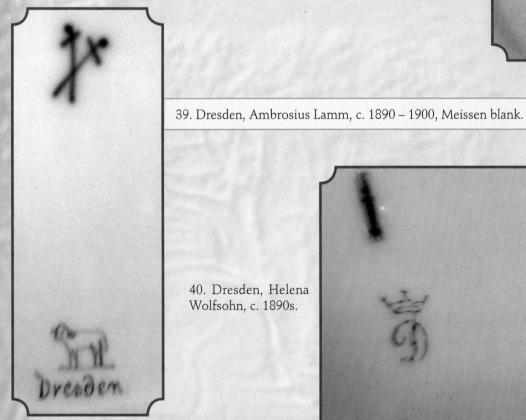

37. Dresden, Carl Thieme, c. 1920s, made for Ovington Bros., NY.

38. Dresden, Heufel & Co., c. 1900 – 1920.

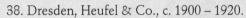

39. Dresden, Ambrosius Lamm, c. 1890 – 1900, Meissen blank.

40. Dresden, Helena Wolfsohn, c. 1890s.

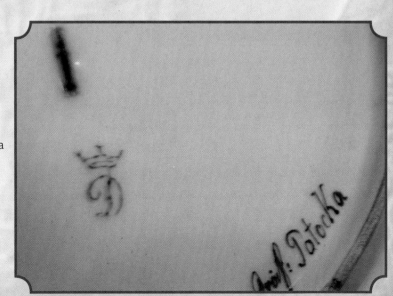

41. Dresden, unidentified decorator, c. 1920s, distributed by A. Schmidt & Sons, NY.

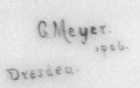

42. Dresden, G. Meyer, c. 1900 – 1910.

43. Dresden, Ambrosius Lamm, c. 1880s (KPM blank).

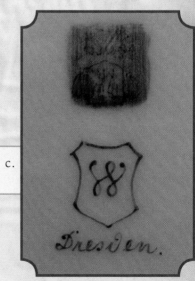

44. Dresden, R. Wehsner, c. 1890s.

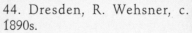

45. Hammersley, c. 1887 – 1912, made for Ovington Bros, NY.

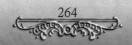

46. Hammersley, c. 1912 – 1939.

47. Heinrich & Co., c. 1911 – 1934 (made for John Wanamaker).

48. Hutschenreuther, c. 1950s.

49. Hutschenreuther, Black Knight, c. 1925 – 1941.

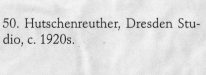

50. Hutschenreuther, Dresden Studio, c. 1920s.

51. Hutschenreuther, Dresden Studio, c. 1918 – 1945.

52. Johnson Bros., c. 1913+.

53. KPM, Berlin, c. 1890 – 1920.

54. KPM, c. 1837 – 1844.

55. KPM, probably outside decorated, c. 1890 – 1900.

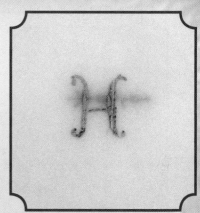

56. KPM, painted outside factory, c. 1890s.

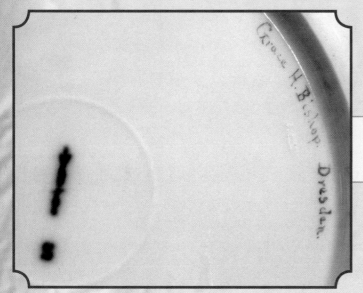

57. KPM, painted outside factory by Dresden decorator Grace H. Bishop, c. 1890s.

58. KPM, Berlin, c. 1900 – 1920.

59. KPM, Berlin, c. 1930 – 1950s.

60. KPM, c. 1837 – 1844.

61. Kutani mark, c. 1890s.

62. Lenox, c. 1906 – 1930, made for Tiffany & Co.

63. Limoges, J. Pouyet, c. 1891 – 1932.

64. Limoges, L. R. L. (Lazeyras, Rosenfeld & Lehman), c. 1920s.

65. Limoges, B & H (Blakeman & Henderson), c. 1890s.

66. Limoges, T & V (Tressemann & Vogt), c. 1892 – 1907.

67. Limoges, Borgfeldt, George, c. 1906 – 1920.

68. Limoges, T & V, c. 1907 – 1919.

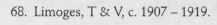

69. Limoges, Klingenberg & Dwenger (decorating mark), c. 1900 – 1910.

70. Limoges, Martin, Charles, c. 1891.

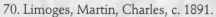

71. Limoges, T & V, two marks, c. 1907 – 1912.

72. Limoges, Guerin, William, c. 1891 – 1900.

73. Limoges, L S & S (Straus, Lewis & Sons), c. 1890 – 1925.

74. Limoges, G. Demartine & Cie, c. 1891 – 1900.

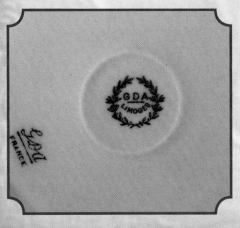

75. Limoges, GDA (Gerard, Dufraisseix & Abbot), c. 1900 – 1941.

76. Limoges, Haviland, c. 1893 – 1930.

77. Limoges, Haviland, c. 1880s, made for Tiffany & Co., NY.

78. Limoges, Delinieres, R., c. 1900 (special Exhibition mark).

79. Limoges, T & V, c. 1892 – 1907 (two marks).

80. Limoges, GDA, c. 1900 – 1941 (two marks).

81. Limoges, Haviland, c. 1876 – 1880.

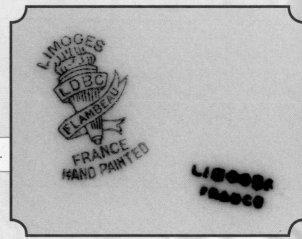

82. Limoges, Flambeau China, c. 1890s – 1915.

83. Limoges, Union Ceramique, c. 1900 – 1938, made for Reizenstein Sons, PA.

84. Limoges, Lanternier, c. 1891 – 1914.

85. Limoges, Raynaud, M., c. 1900.

86. Limoges, Haviland, Charles Field, c. 1882 – 1900.

87. Limoges, Guerin, William & Co., c. 1900 – 1932 (two marks).

88. Lynton Porcelain Co., c. 1982 – present.

89. Meissen, c. 1930 – 1950.

90. Meissen, c. 1850 – 1924.

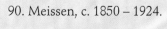

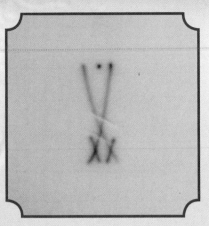

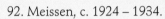
91. Meissen, c. 1924 – 1934, two incised marks.

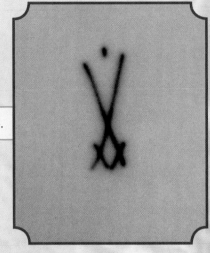

92. Meissen, c. 1924 – 1934.

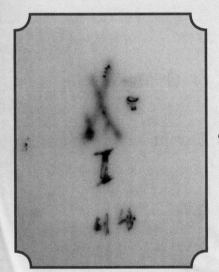

93. Meissen, c. 1830s (first-quality clay).

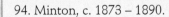
94. Minton, c. 1873 – 1890.

95. Minton, c. 1894, made for T. Goode & Co., London.

96. Minton, c. 1902 – 1911, made for Tiffany & Co., NY.

97. Minton, c. 1873 – 1890, made for T. Goode & Co., London.

98. New Wharf Pottery Co., c. 1890 – 1894.

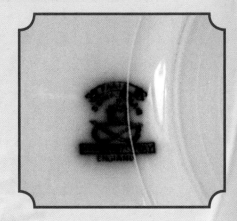

99. Nippon, c. 1891 – 1921.

100. Nippon, c. 1891 – 1921.

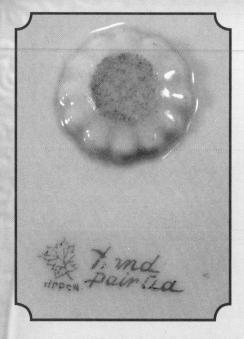

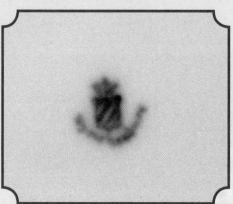

101. Nippon, c. 1891 – 1921.

102. Noritake, c. 1908 – 1911.

103. Nymphenburg, c. 1890 – 1895.

104. Paris, Etienne, J. Fils, c. 1876 – 1890.

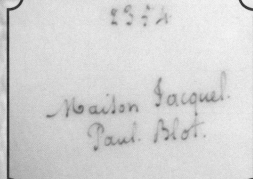

105. Paris, Blot, Paul Studio, c. 1850s.

106. Paris, Lehoche-Pannier, c. 1854 – 1900.

107. Paris, Etienne & Fils Studio, c. 1890 – 1920.

108. Paris, Petit, Jacob, c. 1840 – 1850s.

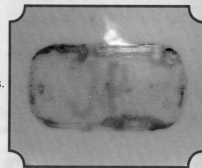

109. Paris, Sevres style, c. 1890s.

110. Paris, LeRosey, Rue de la Paix, c. 1890s.

111. Paris, phony Sevres mark, c. 1868 – 1880.

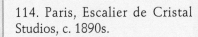

112. Paris, phony Sevres mark, c. 1870 – 1890s.

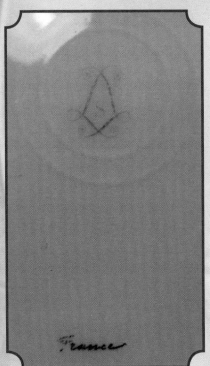

113. Paris, phony Sevres mark, c. 1880 – 1890.

114. Paris, Escalier de Cristal Studios, c. 1890s.

115. Paris, Boyer Studio, c. 1845 – 1850.

116. Paris, LaRoche, Palais Royal, c. 1840s.

117. Paris, Deroche, D. Puchet, c. 1830 – 1850.

118. Paris, Feuillet Studio, c. 1834 – 1855.

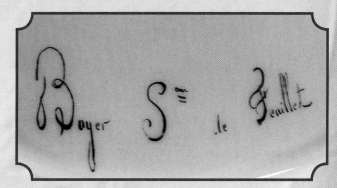

119. Paris, LeRosey, Rue de la Paix, c. 1880s.

120. Paris, unidentified mark, c. 1870s.

121. Pickard, c. 1930 – 1938 (Heinrich & Co. blank).

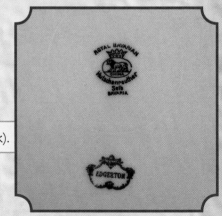

122. Pickard, c. 1925 – 1930.

123. Pickard, c. 1912 – 1918.

124. Pickard, c. 1928 – 1938 (Hutschenreuther blank).

125. Pickard, c. 1919 – 1922.

126. Pirkenhammer (Fischer & Meig), Czechoslo-vakia, c. 1920 – 1945.

127. Pirkenhammer, Austria, c. 1916 – 1918.

128. Rosenthal, c. 1939 – 1945.

129. Rosenthal (Continental Ivory), c. 1945 – 1949.

130. Rosenthal, c. 1891 – 1904.

131. Rosenthal, c. 1898 – 1906.

132. Royal Bayreuth (Sontag & Sons), c. 1887 – 1902.

133. Royal Copenhagen, c. 1922 – present.

134. Royal Copenhagen, c. 1922 – present.

135. Royal Copenhagen, Flora Danica, c. 1960s.

136. Schumann, Carl, c. 1930s.

137. Schumann, Carl, c. 1918.

138. Schumann, Carl, US Zone, c. 1945 – 1949.

139. Schumann, F. A. (Friedrich Adolph), Berlin, c. 1835 – 1869.

140. Sevres, c. 1780s.

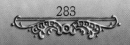

141. Shelley Potteries, c. 1925 – 1940.

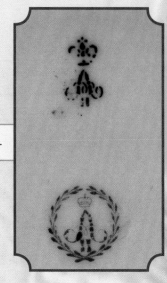

142. St. Petersburg, Imperial Russia, c. 1881 – 1894.

143. Syracuse China, c. 1970s.

144. Teichert, Ernst, Meissen, c. 1884 – 1912.

145. Teichert, Ernst, Meissen, c. 1882 – 1930.

146. Tirschenreuth Porcelain Factory, c. 1960 – 1970s.

147. Ulrich, P. J. Studio, Vienna, c. 1890s.

148. Royal Vienna style, c. 1890s.

149. Royal Vienna style, underglaze blue mark, c. 1880s.

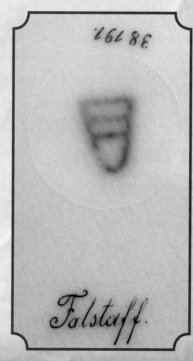

150. Royal Vienna style, c. 1890s.

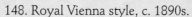

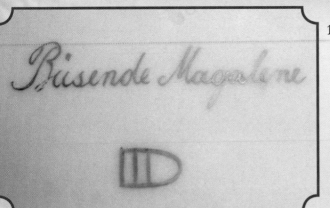

151. Royal Vienna style, c. 1900.

152. Royal Vienna style, c. 1890 – 1920.

153. Royal Vienna style, c. 1890s.

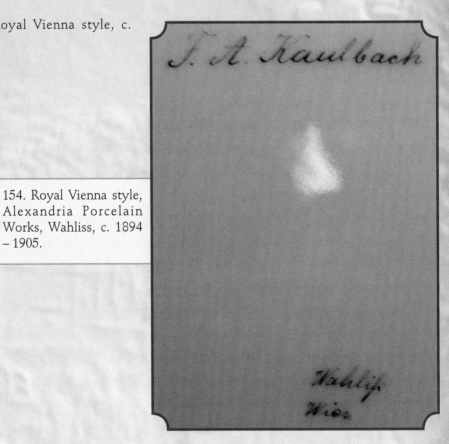

154. Royal Vienna style, Alexandria Porcelain Works, Wahliss, c. 1894 – 1905.

155. Royal Vienna style, red mark, c. 1890s.

156. Volkstedt, Richard Eckert Factory, c. 1894 – 1918.

157. Wedgwood, c. 1878 – 1891.

158. Wheeling Pottery Co., c. 1893 – 1900 (La Belle China mark).

159. Willets Manufacturing Co., c. 1880 – 1904 (brown snake mark).

160. Willets Manufacturing Co., c. 1880 – 1904 (green snake mark).

161. Royal Worcester, c. 1938, made for Mappin & Webb.

162. Royal Worcester, c. 1908, made for Greenleaf & Crosby Co.

163. Royal Worcester, c. 1882.

164. Royal Worcester, c. 1929.

Altman, Seymour and Violet. *The Book of Buffalo Pottery*. Westchester, NY: Schiffer Publishing, Ltd., 1987.

Bagdade, Susan and Al. *Warman's English and Continental Pottery and Porcelain*. Iola, WI: Krause Publications, 1998.

Ballay, Ute. "19th Century Italian Majolica." *Antiques & Collecting*, September 1996.

Bane, Reynolds. "Historical Plates of Staffordshire." *The Antique Trader Annual of Articles Volume V*. Dubuque, IA: Babka Publishing Co., 1976.

Battie, David. *Guide to Understanding 19th and 20th Century British Porcelain*. Woodbridge, England: Antique Collectors' Club, 1994.

Berges, Ruth. *From Gold to Porcelain*. South Brunswick, NJ: Thomas Yoseloff, 1963.

Bergesen, Victoria. *British Ceramics*. London, England: Barrie & Jenkins, 1992.

Bischoff, Ilse. "Vigee-LeBrun and the Women of the French Court." *Antiques*, November 1967.

Brown, Peter. "Derby Porcelain: The Work of Floral and Botanical Artists, 1790 – 1805." LookSmart's Find Articles. http://www.findarticles.com/p/articles/mi_m1026/is_6_163/ai_102654405/print

Buchan, Vivian. "The Royalty of Royal Copenhagen." *The Antique Trader Annual of Articles Volume VI*, Dubuque, IA: Babka Publishing Co., 1977.

Charleston, Robert J. *World Ceramics*. Secaucus, NJ: Chartwell Books, Inc., 1977.

Collector's Information Bureau. *Collectibles Market Guide and Price Index*. Barrington, IL: Collector's Information Bureau, 1995.

Danckert, Ludwig. *Directory of European Porcelain*. London, England: N.A.G. Press, Ltd., 1981.

Davidson, Michael Worth. *Everyday Life through the Ages*. Pleasantville, NY: The Reader's Digest Association, Inc., 1992.

Devanney, Joseph J. "Great Imitators." *Antique Trader*, August 1, 2004.

Eberlein, Harold and Ramsdell, Roger. *The Practical Book of Chinaware*. New York, NY: J. B. Lippincott Co., 1948.

Engelbreit, Mary. *Plates*. Kansas City, MO: Andrew McMeel Publishing, 1994.

Faÿ-Hallé, Antoinette, and Barbara Mundt. *Porcelain of the Nineteenth Century*. New York, NY: Rizzoli, 1983.

Field, Rachael. *MacDonald Guide to Buying Antique Pottery & Porcelain*. Radnor, PA: Wallace-Homestead Co., 1987.

Fisher, Stanley. *Worcester Porcelain*. London, England: Ward Lock & Company, Ltd., 1970.

Flayderman, Norman, and Edna Lagerwall. *Collecting Tomorrow's Antiques Today*. New York, NY: Doubleday & Co., 1972.

Forrest, Tim. *The Bullfinch Anatomy of Antique China and Silver*. London, England: Marshall Editions, 1998.

Gaston, Mary Frank. *The Collector's Encyclopedia of Limoges Porcelain*, 1st, 2nd, and 3rd eds. Paducah, KY: Collector Books, 1980, 1992, 2000.

Glauser, Frederick. "European Portrait Painting on Porcelain." *The Journal of Antiques & Collectibles*, August 2005.

Godden, Geoffrey. *Encyclopedia of British Pottery and Porcelain Marks*. London, England: Barrie & Jenkins, 1986, 1991.

_____. *Godden's Guide to English Porcelain*. Radnor, PA: Wallace-Homestead, 1992.

_____. *Godden's Guide to European Porcelains*. New York, NY: Cross River Press, 1993.

Goldblum, Nettie. "American Belleek." *The Antique Trader Annual of Articles Volume V*, 1976.

Goldstein, Doris. "Joyful Majolica." *Art & Antiques*, January 2004.

Grandjean, Bredo L. *Flora Danica*. Copenhagen, Denmark: Hassing Publisher, 1950.

de Guillebon, Regine de Plinval. *Paris Porcelain 1770 – 1850*. London, England: Barrie & Jenkins, 1972.

Harran, Jim and Susan. *Collectible Cups & Saucers* books *I*, *II*, and *III*. Paducah, KY: Collector Books, 1998 – 2003.

_____. *Dresden Porcelain Studios*. Paducah, KY: Collector Books, 2002.

_____. *Meissen Porcelain*. Paducah, KY: Collector Books, 2006.

Hawke, Sandra. "Collectors Favor Hand-Painted China Pieces." Spring 2002 Home Improvement Show. http://www.billingsgazette.com/special/s002homeshow/collectors.html

Hudgeons, Thomas. *Official Price Guide to Collector Plates*. Orlando, FL: The House of Collectibles, 1982.

Huxford, Sharon and Bob. *Schroeder's Antiques Price Guide* 27th ed. Paducah, KY: Collector Books, 2007.

Jones, Vere. "Royal Worcester." *Antique Trader Weekly*, September 22, 1993.

Kamm, Dorothy. "Designing Women." *Antique Trader Weekly*, September 1995.

Karsnitz, Jim and Vivian. *Oyster Plates*. Schiffer Publishing, Ltd., Atglen, PA: Schiffer Publishing, 1993.

Katz-Marks, Marianne. *Majolica Pottery*, series 1 and 2. Paducah, KY: Collector Books, 1983, 1986.

Keefe, John W. "The Porcelains of Paris, 1770 – 1870." *Antiques*, February 1996.

Kovel, Ralph and Terry. *Kovels' New Dictionary of Marks*. New York, NY: Crown Publishers, Inc., 1986.

Kozin, Betty and Gene. "Royal Worcester Porcelain." *The Antique Trader Annual of Articles Vol. VI*. Dubuque, IA: Babka Publishing Co., 1977.

Ledes, Allison Eckardt. "Redoute's Flowers." LookSmart's Find Articles. http://www.findarticles.com/p/articles/mi_m/026/is_1_162/ai_88825932

Lehner, Lois. *Lehner's Encyclopedia of U. S. Marks on Pottery, Porcelain & Clay*. Paducah, KY: Collector Books, 1988.

Lynd, Mitch. "Great Moments in Apple History." Midwest Apple Improvement Association. http://www.hort.purdue.edu/newcrop/maia/history.html

MacFall, Haldane, *Vigee Le Brun*. New York, NY: Frederick A. Stokes, 1922.

Mackay, James. *An Encyclopedia of Small Antiques*. New York, NY: Harper & Row, 1975.

Martinsen, Paul T. "Royal Copenhagen Christmas Plates." *Christmas*, 1957.

McClinton, Katherine Morrison. "Royal Doulton Rack Plates and Limited Editions." *The Antique Trader Annual of Articles Volume IX*, Dubuque, IA: Babka Publishing Co., 1978.

Miller, Judith. *Miller's Antiques Encyclopedia*. London: Reed Consumer Book, Ltd., 1998.

Murray, Michael D. *European Majolica*. Atglen, PA: Schiffer Publishing, Ltd., 1997.

Osborne, Charles. "Majolica Flamboyant Victorian Ware." *The Encyclopedia of Collectibles*. Time-Life Books, 1979.

Perkins, Fredda. "Marvelous Majolica." Country Collector. www.countrycollector.com/majolica

Ramsey, L. G. *The Concise Encyclopedia of Antiques Volume Four Connoisseur*. New York, NY: Hawthorn Books, Inc., 1959.

Ray, Marcia. *Collectible Ceramics*. New York: Crown Publishers, Inc., 1974.

Reed, Alan B. *Collector's Encyclopedia of Pickard China*. Paducah, KY: Collector Books, 1995.

Rendall, Richard, and Elise Abrams. *Hand Painted Porcelain Plates, Nineteenth Century to the Present*. Atglen, PA: Schiffer Publishing, Ltd., 2003.

Richman, Irwin. "Collecting Italian Majolica." *Antiques & Auction News*, April 5, 1996.

Röntgen, Robert E. *Marks on German, Bohemian & Austrian Porcelain*. Exton, PA: Schiffer Publishing, Ltd., 1981.

Root & deRochemont. *Eating in America*. New York: William Morrow & Co., 1976.

Roren, Melva. "Denmark's Christmas Gifts" and "Danish Blue." *Christmas*, 1962 and 1969.

Royal Copenhagen, Ltd. *Flora Danica*. Copenhagen, Denmark: Royal Copenhagen, Ltd., 1989.

Schalten, Frito T. "The Variety of Decoration on Dutch Delft, 1625 – 1675." *Antiques*, January 1995.

Schiffer, Nancy N. "Exquisite Imari." *Art & Antiques*, February 2004.

Scott, Joseph. "Charger Plates Made a Comeback." *The Daily Item*, October 10, 2004.

Simpson, Richard. "Oyster Plates." *Antiques & Collecting,* June 1997.

Snodgrass, Ginni D. "Keramika a Porcelan Cesky-Bohemsky." Fakes & Frauds Parts I and II. http://www.ginni.com/collection/fakes.html

Snyder, Jeffrey B, and Leslie Bockol. *Majolica American & European Wares.* Atglen, PA: Schiffer Publishing Company, Ltd., 1994.

Stefano, Frank Jr. "Wedgwood Old Blue Historical Plates." *The Antique Trader Annual of Articles Volume VI,* Dubuque, IA: Babka Publishing Co., 1977.

Twitchett, John, and Betty Bailey. *Royal Crown Derby.* Woodbridge, England: Antique Collectors' Club, Ltd., 1976.

Van Patten, Joan. *The Collector's Encyclopedia of Nippon Porcelain,* vols. 2 and 3. Paducah, KY: Collector Books, 1982.

Verbeten, Sharon Korbeck. "Beyond the Blues." *Antique Trader,* May 25, 2005.

Ware, George W. *German and Austrian Porcelain.* New York, NY: Crown Publishers, 1963.

Wilkinson, Vega. *Spode-Copeland-Spode.* Woodbridge, England: Antique Collectors' Club, Ltd., 2002.

Williams, Barbara Sachett. "Buffalo Pottery: A Premium Investment. " My Antique Mall. http://www.myantiquewall.com/Aqstories/Buffalo.htmls

Wood, Robin. "A History of the Wooden Plate." Robin Wood History Articles. http://www.robin.wood.co.uk./histframe.htm

_____. "World Cultures." The British Museum. http://www.thebritishmuseum.ac.uk/compass/ixbin/print?0BJ3740

_____. "China and Porcelain." OldandSold Antiques Auction & Marketplace. http://www.oldandsold.com/articles03/china5.shtml

_____. *Christmas in Denmark.* Chicago, IL: World Book, Inc., 1986.

_____. Creative Quotations. http://www.creativequotations.com.

_____. "Dinnerware." Royal Copenhagen. http://www.royalco penhagen.com

_____. E-Limoges. http://e-limoges.com/makers

_____. "Franz Xaver Thallmaier." AntiqForum. http://www.antiqforum.com/lib_KPM_Franz-Xavier_Thallmaier.html

_____. "History of Plates." Lockside Antiques. http://www.mysite.wanadoo-members.co.uk/lockside_antiques/page6.html

_____. "History of Trenton Pottery Making." The Trenton Museum. http://www.ellarslie.org/about_pottery.htm.

_____. "An Introduction to Samian Pottery." *New Archaeology.* http://www.newarchaeology.com/articles/samian.shtm

_____. "Landscape." *Wikipedia, The Free Encyclopedia.* http://en.wikipedia.org/wiki/Landscape

_____. "Lynton Porcelain — Fine English Bone China." The Lynton Mill Group. http://www.lynton-group.co.uk/history.htm.

_____. "Samian Ware." Swansea Heriage http://www.swanseaheritage.net/article/got.asp?ARTICLE_ID=648PRIMARY-THEME.ID=5

_____. "Sarreguemines." Out of Brussels Antiques & Artwork. http://www.outofbrusselsantiques.com/majolica-manufacturers.htm

_____. "A Short History of Collectible Plates." World Collectors Net. http://www.worldcollectorsnet.com/magazine/issue14/iss/4p4.html

_____. "Still Life." National Gallery of Art: Themes in American Art. http://www.nga.gov/education/america/still.shtm

_____. "Trencher." *Encyclopedia Britannica.* http://www.britannica.com/eb/article-9073297

_____. "Vieux Paris Porcelain." *Antiques Digest.* http://www.oldandsold.com/articles/article372.shtml

_____. "Why Are Cakes Round?" The Food Timeline: History Notes — Cake. http://www.foodtimeline.org/foodcakes.html

INDEX

MEISSEN PORCELAIN

This beautiful book features everyday items available in the marketplace, not the eighteenth century museum pieces found in many Meissen books. The majority of pieces featured date from the mid-nineteenth century through the 1950s. More than 625 color photos are included, along with a helpful marks section. The book includes chapters on decorative porcelain, flower painting, Oriental motifs, Meissen's famous Blue Onion pattern, figures, copycats, and other useful information. 2006 values.

Item #6835 • ISBN: 978-1-57432-474-7 • 8¹/₂ x 11 • 208 pgs. • HB • $29.95

Other books by

Jim and Susan Harran

COLLECTIBLE
CUPS & SAUCERS

These books are divided into several collectible categories: early years (1700 – 1875), cabinet cups, nineteenth and twentieth century European and American dinnerware, English bone china and earthenware cups and saucers, miniatures, mustache cups, and more. Book III also contains two brand new categories: Japanese cups and saucers and art glass cups and saucers made by the leading glass factories in Europe and the U.S. Over 800 color photos fill Book II, and Book III boasts over 1,000 photos! And there are no repeats in any volume! Each book includes a thorough marks section. Owners of these books will learn about the history of tea, coffee, and cups and saucers, as well as how cups and saucers were made and decorated, manufacturers' information, and other pertinent facts.

Book II · Item #5529 · ISBN: 978-1-57432-155-5 · 8½ x 11 360 pgs. · PB · 2004 values · $19.95
Book III · Item #6326 · ISBN: 978-1-57432-352-8 · 8½ x 11 384 pgs. · PB · 2007 values · $24.95

more greatTITLES from collector books

DOLLS

6315 **American Character Dolls**, Izen $24.95
7346 **Barbie Doll** Around the World, 1964 – 2007, Augustyniak $29.95
2079 **Barbie Doll** Fashion, Volume I, Eames $24.95
4846 **Barbie Doll** Fashion, Volume II, Eames $24.95
6319 **Barbie Doll** Fashion, Volume III, Eames $29.95
6546 Collector's Ency. of **Barbie** Doll Exclusives & More, 3rd Ed., Augustyniak $29.95
6920 Collector's Encyclopedia of American **Composition Dolls**, Volume I, Mertz.. $29.95
6451 Collector's Encyclopedia of American **Composition Dolls**, Volume II, Mertz. $29.95
6636 Collector's Encyclopedia of **Madame Alexander Dolls**, Crowsey.............. $24.95
6456 Collector's Guide to **Dolls of the 1960s and 1970s**, Volume II, Sabulis $24.95
6944 The Complete Guide to **Shirley Temple** Dolls and Collectibles, Bervaldi-Camaratta .. $29.95
7028 **Doll Values**, Antique to Modern, 9th Edition, Edward...................... $14.95
6467 **Paper Dolls** of the 1960s, 1970s, and 1980s, Nichols.................... $24.95
6642 20th Century **Paper Dolls**, Young....................................... $19.95

TOYS & MARBLES

2333 Antique & Collectible **Marbles**, 3rd Edition, Grist $9.95
6649 Big Book of **Toy Airplanes**, Miller...................................... $24.95
6938 Everett Grist's Big Book of **Marbles**, 3rd Edition $24.95
7523 **Breyer Animal** Collector's Gde., 5th Ed., Browell/Korber-Weimer/Kesicki. $24.95
6633 **Hot Wheels**, The Ultimate Redline Guide, 2nd Ed., Clark/Wicker $29.95
6466 **Matchbox Toys**, 1947 to 2003, 4th Edition, Johnson...................... $24.95
6840 **Schroeder's Collectible Toys**, Antique to Modern Price Guide, 10th Ed. $17.95
6638 The Other **Matchbox Toys**, 1947 to 2004, Johnson........................ $19.95
6650 **Toy Car** Collector's Guide, 2nd Edition, Johnson $24.95

JEWELRY, WATCHES & PURSES

4704 Antique & Collectible **Buttons**, Wisniewski $19.95
4850 Collectible **Costume Jewelry**, Simonds $24.95
5675 Collectible **Silver Jewelry**, Rezazadeh $24.95
6468 Collector's Ency. of Pocket & Pendant **Watches**, 1500 – 1950, Bell......... $24.95
6554 **Coro Jewelry**, Brown.. $29.95
7529 **Costume Jewelry** 101, 2nd Edition, Carroll............................. $24.95
7025 **Costume Jewelry** 202, Carroll $24.95
4940 **Costume Jewelry**, A Practical Handbook & Value Guide, Rezazadeh $24.95
6027 The **Estée Lauder** Solid Perfume Compact Collection, Gerson.............. $24.95
5812 Fifty Years of Collectible **Fashion Jewelry**, 1925 – 1975, Baker $24.95
6330 **Handkerchiefs**: A Collector's Guide, Guarnaccia/Guggenheim $24.95
6833 **Handkerchiefs**: A Collector's Guide, Volume II, Guarnaccia/Guggenheim .. $24.95
6464 Inside the **Jewelry** Box, Pitman $24.95
7358 Inside the **Jewelry** Box, Volume 2, Pitman $24.95
5695 **Ladies' Vintage Accessories**, Johnson $24.95
1181 100 Years of Collectible **Jewelry**, 1850 – 1950, Baker $9.95
6645 100 Years of **Purses**, 1880s to 1980s, Aikins $24.95
6942 **Rhinestone Jewelry**: Figurals, Animals, and Whimsicals, Brown $24.95

ARTIFACTS, GUNS, KNIVES, & TOOLS

1868 Antique **Tools**, Our American Heritage, McNerney $9.95
6822 **Antler, Bone & Shell** Artifacts, Hothem................................ $24.95
1426 **Arrowheads & Projectile Points**, Hothem $7.95
5355 **Cattaraugus Cutlery** Co., Stewart/Ritchie $19.95
6231 **Indian Artifacts** of the Midwest, Book V, Hothem $24.95
7037 **Modern Guns**, Identification & Values, 16th Ed., Quertermous $16.95
7034 **Ornamental Indian Artifacts**, Hothem $34.95
6567 **Paleo-Indian Artifacts**, Hothem....................................... $29.95
6569 **Remington Knives**, Past & Present, Stewart/Ritchie $16.95
7366 Standard Guide to **Razors**, 3rd Edition, Stewart/Ritchie $12.95
7035 Standard **Knife** Collector's Guide, 5th Edition, Ritchie/Stewart $16.95

PAPER COLLECTIBLES & BOOKS

6623 Collecting **American Paintings**, James $29.95
7039 Collecting **Playing Cards**, Pickvet $24.95
6826 Collecting Vintage **Children's Greeting Cards**, McPherson $24.95
6553 Collector's Guide to **Cookbooks**, Daniels.............................. $24.95
1441 Collector's Guide to **Post Cards**, Wood $9.95
6627 Early 20th Century **Hand-Painted Photography**, Ivankovich.............. $24.95
6936 **Leather Bound Books**, Boutiette $24.95
7036 **Old Magazine Advertisements**, 1890 – 1950, Clear $24.95
6940 **Old Magazines**, 2nd Edition, Clear.................................... $19.95
3973 **Sheet Music** Reference & Price Guide, 2nd Ed., Pafik/Guiheen $19.95
6837 Vintage **Postcards** for the Holidays, 2nd Edition, Reed................. $24.95

GLASSWARE

6930 Anchor Hocking's **Fire-King** & More, 3rd Ed., Florence $24.95
7524 Coll. **Glassware from the 40s, 50s & 60s**, 9th Edition, Florence $19.95
6921 Collector's Encyclopedia of **American Art Glass**, 2nd Edition, Shuman $29.95
7526 Collector's Encyclopedia of **Depression Glass**, 18th Ed., Florence $19.95
3905 Collector's Encyclopedia of **Milk Glass**, Newbound $24.95
7026 Colors in **Cambridge Glass** II, Natl. Cambridge Collectors, Inc.......... $29.95
7029 **Elegant Glassware** of the Depression Era, 12th Edition, Florence $24.95
6334 Encyclopedia of **Paden City Glass**, Domitz $29.95
3981 Evers' Standard **Cut Glass** Value Guide $12.95
6126 **Fenton Art Glass**, 1907 – 1939, 2nd Ed., Whitmyer..................... $29.95
6628 **Fenton Glass** Made for Other Companies, Domitz $29.95
7030 **Fenton Glass** Made for Other Companies, Volume II, Domitz.............. $29.95
6462 Florences' **Glass Kitchen Shakers**, 1930 – 1950s $19.95

COSTUME JEWELRY & PURSES

6039 Signed Beauties of **Costume Jewelry**, Brown $24.95
6341 Signed Beauties of **Costume Jewelry**, Volume II, Brown $24.95
6555 20th Century **Costume Jewelry**, Aikins $24.95
5620 Unsigned Beauties of **Costume Jewelry**, Brown $24.95
4878 Vintage & Contemporary **Purse Accessories**, Gerson $24.95

5042 Florences' **Glassware Pattern Identification** Guide, Vol. I $18.95
5615 Florences' **Glassware Pattern Identification** Guide, Vol. II $19.95
6643 Florences' **Glassware Pattern Identification** Guide, Vol. IV $19.95
6641 Florences' **Ovenware** from the 1920s to the Present $24.95
6226 **Fostoria** Value Guide, Long/Seate $19.95
6127 The **Glass Candlestick** Book, Volume 1, Akro Agate to Fenton, Felt/Stoer .. $24.95
6228 The **Glass Candlestick** Book, Volume 2, Fostoria to Jefferson, Felt/Stoer . $24.95
6461 The **Glass Candlestick** Book, Volume 3, Kanawha to Wright, Felt/Stoer ... $29.95
6648 Glass **Toothpick Holders**, 2nd Edition, Bredehoft/Sanford.................... $29.95
5827 **Kitchen Glassware** of the Depression Years, 6th Edition, Florence $24.95
6133 **Mt. Washington Art Glass**, Sisk $49.95
7027 Pocket Guide to **Depression Glass** & More, 15th Edition, Florence $12.95
6925 Standard Encyclopedia of **Carnival Glass**, 10th Ed., Edwards/Carwile $29.95
6926 Standard **Carnival Glass** Price Guide, 15th Ed., Edwards/Carwile $9.95
6566 Standard Encyclopedia of **Opalescent Glass**, 5th Ed., Edwards/Carwile ... $29.95
7364 Standard Encyclopedia of **Pressed Glass**, 5th Ed., Edwards/Carwile $29.95
6476 **Westmoreland Glass**, The Popular Years, 1940 – 1985, Kovar $29.95

POTTERY

6922 **American Art Pottery**, 2nd Edition, Sigafoose $24.95
5529 Collectible **Cups & Saucers**, Book II, Harran $19.95
6326 Collectible **Cups & Saucers**, Book III, Harran $24.95
6331 Collecting **Head Vases**, Barron $24.95
6943 Collecting **Royal Copley**, Devine... $19.95
6621 Collector's Encyclopedia of **American Dinnerware**, 2nd Ed., Cunningham .$29.95
5034 Collector's Encyclopedia of **California Pottery**, 2nd Ed., Chipman $24.95
6629 Collector's Encyclopedia of **Fiesta**, 10th Ed., Huxford......................... $24.95
3431 Collector's Encyclopedia of **Homer Laughlin China**, Jasper $24.95
1276 Collector's Encyclopedia of **Hull Pottery**, Roberts $19.95
5609 Collector's Encyclopedia of **Limoges Porcelain**, 3rd Ed., Gaston $29.95
6637 Collector's Encyclopedia of **Made in Japan Ceramics**, First Ed., White $24.95
5677 Collector's Encyclopedia of **Niloak**, 2nd Edition, Gifford $29.95
5841 Collector's Encyclopedia of **Roseville Pottery**, Vol. 1, Huxford/Nickel $24.95
5842 Collector's Encyclopedia of **Roseville Pottery**, Vol. 2, Huxford/Nickel...... $24.95
6646 Collector's Ency. of **Stangl Artware, Lamps, and Birds**, 2nd Ed., Runge .. $29.95
3314 Collector's Encyclopedia of **Van Briggle Art Pottery**, Sasicki $24.95
6634 Collector's Ultimate Ency. of **Hull Pottery**, Volume 1, Roberts $29.95
6829 The Complete Guide to **Corning Ware & Visions Cookware**, Coroneos...... $19.95
7530 Decorative **Plates**, Harran $29.95
5918 Florences' Big Book of **Salt & Pepper Shakers** $24.95
6320 Gaston's **Blue Willow**, 3rd Edition $19.95
6630 Gaston's **Flow Blue China**, The Comprehensive Guide.......................... $29.95
7021 Hansons' American **Art Pottery** Collection.. $29.95
7032 **Head Vases**, 2nd Edition, Cole.. $24.95
2379 Lehner's Ency. of **U.S. Marks** on Pottery, Porcelain & China $24.95
4722 **McCoy Pottery** Collector's Reference & Value Guide, Hanson/Nissen $19.95
5913 **McCoy Pottery**, Volume III, Hanson/Nissen $24.95

6835 **Meissen** Porcelain, Harran $29.95
7536 The Official **Precious Moments**® Collector's Guide to Figurines, 3rd Ed., Bomm ..$19.95
6335 Pictorial Guide to **Pottery & Porcelain Marks**, Lage $29.95
1440 **Red Wing Stoneware**, DePasquale/Peck/Peterson $9.95
6838 **R.S. Prussia** & More, McCaslin $29.95
6945 **TV Lamps** to Light the World, Shuman $29.95
7043 **Uhl Pottery**, 2nd Edition, Feldmeyer/Holtzman.................................. $16.95
6828 The Ultimate Collector's Encyclopedia of **Cookie Jars**, Roerig $29.95
6640 Van Patten's ABC's of Collecting **Nippon Porcelain** $29.95

OTHER COLLECTIBLES

6446 Antique & Contemporary **Advertising Memorabilia**, 2nd Edition, Summers . $29.95
6935 Antique **Golf Collectibles**, Georgiady.. $29.95
1880 Antique **Iron**, McNerney $9.95
6622 The Art of American **Game Calls**, Lewis $24.95
6551 The Big Book of **Cigarette Lighters**, Flanagan $29.95
7024 B.J. Summers' Guide to **Coca-Cola**, 6th Edition $29.95
1128 **Bottle** Pricing Guide, 3rd Ed., Cleveland $7.95
6924 Captain John's **Fishing Tackle** Price Guide, 2nd Edition, Kolbeck.............. $24.95
6342 Collectible **Soda Pop** Memorabilia, Summers $24.95
6625 Collector's Encyclopedia of **Bookends**, Kuritzky/De Costa $29.95
5666 Collector's Encyclopedia of **Granite Ware**, Book 2, Greguire $29.95
6928 Early **American Furniture**, Obbard $19.95
7042 The Ency. of Early American & Antique **Sewing Machines**, 3rd Ed., Bays ... $29.95
6561 Field Guide to **Fishing Lures**, Lewis $16.95
7031 **Fishing Lure** Collectibles, An Ency. of the Early Years, Murphy/Edmisten .. $29.95
7350 **Flea Market Trader**, 16th Edition $15.95
6458 **Fountain Pens**, Past & Present, 2nd Edition, Erano $24.95
7352 **Garage Sale** & Flea Market Annual, 15th Edition $19.95
3906 **Heywood-Wakefield** Modern Furniture, Rouland $18.95
7033 **Hot Kitchen** & Home Collectibles of the 30s, 40s, and 50s, Zweig......... $24.95
2216 **Kitchen Antiques**, 1790 – 1940, McNerney $14.95
7038 The Marketplace Guide to **Oak Furniture**, 2nd Edition, Blundell............... $29.95
6639 **McDonald's Drinkware**, Kelly $24.95
6939 Modern Collectible **Tins**, 2nd Edition, McPherson............................... $24.95
6832 Modern **Fishing Lure** Collectibles, Volume 4, Lewis $24.95
7349 Modern **Fishing Lure** Collectibles, Volume 5, Lewis $29.95
6322 Pictorial Guide to **Christmas Ornaments** & Collectibles, Johnson $29.95
6842 Raycrafts' **Americana** Price Guide & DVD $19.95
7538 **Schroeder's Antiques** Price Guide, 26th Edition $17.95
6038 **Sewing Tools** & Trinkets, Volume 2, Thompson $24.95
5007 **Silverplated Flatware**, Revised 4th Edition, Hagan $18.95
7367 **Star Wars** Super Collector's Wish Book, 4th Edition, Carlton $29.95
7537 **Summers'** Pocket Guide to **Coca-Cola**, 6th Edition $14.95
6841 Vintage **Fabrics**, Gridley/Kiplinger/McClure $19.95
6036 Vintage **Quilts**, Aug/Newman/Roy $24.95
6941 The Wonderful World of Collecting **Perfume Bottles**, Flanagan $29.95

| News for Collectors | Request a Catalog | Meet the Authors | Find Newest Releases | Calendar of Events | Special Sale Items |

www.collectorbooks.com

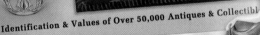